READING
THE BIBLE
FOR THE LOVE
OF GOD

READING
THE BIBLE
FOR THE LOVE
OF GOD

ALAN REYNOLDS

Brazos Press
A Division of Baker Book House Co
Grand Rapids, Michigan 49516

Published by Brazos Press
a division of Baker Book House Company
P.O. Box 6287, Grand Rapids, MI 49516-6287
www.brazospress.com

Printed in the United States of America

Library of Congress Cataloging-in-Publication Data
Reynolds, Alan, 1930–
    Reading the Bible for the love of God / Alan Reynolds.
        p.   cm.
    Includes bibliographical references.
    ISBN 1-58743-082-7 (pbk.)
    1. Bible—Reading. I. Title.
BS617.R49 2003
220'.071—dc21   2003009269

Published in association with the literary agency of Alive Communications, Inc., 7680 Goddard Street, Suite 200, Colorado Springs, Colorado 80920.

CONTENTS

ACKNOWLEDGMENTS

The thoughts contained in this book come after a lifetime of pondering. For most of my life I have been a pastor. Of necessity then, I have been a generalist rather than a specialist, trying to understand the world in which I live and trying to see the significance of the Christian faith in the context of this world.

I would like to thank literary agent, Kathy Helmers, who through Eugene Peterson's intervention, has believed in this work and has given it her personal attention beyond mere professional interest. She has become a true friend in Christ. I would also like to thank Eugene Peterson, soul-friend, for writing the foreword to this book.

There are many other people whom I would like to thank for helping in the production of this book, including my wife, Brenda, who has borne with me the thrill of love and the pain of living for over forty years. I want to thank several people who assisted me by reading and providing helpful criticism— Derek Pinton, John Palmer, George Stanford, Ambury Stuart, John Culter, Lloyd and Margaret Skarsgard, David Ley, and my pastor, Ed Searcy. I am honored by the careful reading they gave to the manuscript; their many helpful suggestions have contributed significantly to an improved work.

I wish to thank, especially, Arla Pinton, a member of my congregation—University Hill Congregation on the campus of the University of British Columbia in Vancouver. Arla has been a notable help and support through the last fifteen years of my ministry, and has continued to encourage me to seek publication despite many discouragements. Without her encouragement and support, this work would never have been written.

Now I turn this work over to you who read it. "In simple humility, let our gardener, God, landscape you with the Word, making a salvation-garden of your life" (James 1:21 THE MESSAGE).

Alan Reynolds

Would you know our Lord's meaning in all this?
Learn it well.
Love was the meaning.
Who showed it to you? Love.
What did God show you? Love.
Why did God show it to you? For love.
Hold fast to this and you shall learn and know more about love.
But you shall never learn anything except love from God.
So I taught that love was our Lord's meaning.
And I saw full surely that before ever God made us,
God loved us.
This love was never quenched, nor ever shall be.
And in this love God has created everything that is.
And in his love God has made all things for our benefit.
And in this love is our life everlasting.
And all this shall we see in God without end—
which Jesus grant us.
Amen.

The final written words of Julian of Norwich in Ralph Milton, *Julian's Cell: The Earthy Story of Julian of Norwich* (Northstone: Kelowna, British Columbia, 2002), p. 191.

9

FOREWORD

The near universal literacy that is a feature of Western civilization was fueled in large part because our ancestors believed it was essential that people be able to read the Bible. Novelist Marilynne Robinson has observed that "all the immeasurable practical benefits that came with mass literacy, its spectacular utility, awaited this unworldly stimulus."

The literacy skills adequate for reading the Bible that by now have been acquired by virtually everybody ten years and older in North America is matched by easily available Bibles to read. The printing technology that made it possible to mass publish books and magazines and newspapers was also motivated by the conviction that it was essential that everyone have a Bible to read. Anybody now who wants a Bible can have one. If you can't afford to buy a Bible, there are any number of people around who will give you one. Is there any other book of which that can be said on the same scale?

The ability to read and the availability of books to read, two fundamental features of our culture that we take for granted, both had their origin in the conviction that reading the Bible and having a Bible to read were nonnegotiable human essentials.

And now we are faced with this astonishing irony: everybody (I exaggerate slightly) can read, everybody has a Bible (again, a slight exaggeration), and yet so much of the reading is misreading and many of the Bibles are unread (not an exaggeration). How has it come to pass that the enormous success in achieving mass literacy so that everyone can read the Bible and the technological invention that revolutionized printing so that everyone can have a Bible to read has resulted in such widespread biblical illiteracy? I have been keeping close company with pastors and teachers for fifty years and know from decades of conversations, confirmed by my own experience, that most of them, dismayed by the marginal place of the Bible among the people under their care, consider it one of their primary tasks to guide the men and women, children and youth in their sanctuaries and classrooms not only to read the Bible but to read it rightly. They know this is necessary and embrace the work. But they also find it surprisingly and unendingly difficult.

This seems exceedingly odd, for the Bible was not written for an intellectual and learned upper class. It is not a difficult book that only "smart" people can get. In fact, most of the first "readers" of the Bible couldn't read; they listened to it being read by one of the rare ones in the community who could read. They were stonemasons, housewives, grapepickers, fishermen, the outcasts and unemployed. This was not a book to be studied at a desk in a schoolroom; this was a book to be listened to and *lived*. It was not a book valued because it held tons of information that could be looked up and used; it was a book that formed their understanding of who they were and who God is. As they listened to the words, they experienced the words as written (spoken) personally to them; their lives were formed in trust and love, hope and obedience. They didn't *know* more, they *became* more.

And perhaps that is the clue to why so much contemporary Bible reading is disappointing. The schools in which we all learn to read teach us to read for information and for performance; we learn to read so that we can know things and do things. Our schools do this very well and the results show it: we know a lot, we can do a lot. But these reading habits are so deeply ingrained in us that it is difficult to shift gears and *listen* to the text personally, listening in a participatory and responsive way to words that convey God's gospel, evoking our faith and love in return.

Reading the Bible doesn't require any great technical skills, but it does require a radical shift from our habitual reading-for-information to personal reading-as-listening. This shift turns out to be far more difficult than just learning how to read in the first place or getting together enough money to buy a Bible. And that may very well be why our ancestors had an advantage over us— their Bible reading/listening took place entirely in a context of personal relationships in which they were immersed in common work. The Bible was not *about,* it was *for:* for *you.*

Alan Reynolds is one of the pastors I mentioned earlier, a pastor who has spent a vocational lifetime in guiding people in all matters of Bible reading. He is a skilled pastor and guide, richly experienced in his understandings of the ways that the culture we have assimilated (and sometimes our own contrariness—one friend calls it "lunging for isolated verses") so often messes up our Bible reading, and patient in his gentle but incisive direction in reading the Bible rightly. Rightly, of course, means "for you." Now that we can all read and all of us have Bibles, the next thing is that we relearn what was simply assumed for so many of the generations that preceded us—that we learn to read rightly.

Eugene H. Peterson, author of
The Message: The Bible in Contemporary Language

1

A NEW WAY
OF READING THE BIBLE

Beyond the Thumpers
and the Bashers

The Bible is not an "object" for us to study but a partner with whom we may dialogue. It is usual in our modern world to regard any "thing" as an object which will yield its secrets to us if we are diligent and discerning. . . . Reading the Bible requires that we abandon the subject-object way of perceiving things. It requires that we give up the notion of the Bible as a "book" to be acted upon, analyzed, studied, and interpreted. Perhaps it will help if we give up thinking of it as a "book" and regard it as a "tradition" which continues to be alive and surging among us.

Walter Brueggemann[1]

D o not let go of the Bible until it blesses you." When Old Testament scholar Phyllis Trible spoke these words to a conference of preachers in Montreat, North Carolina, in June 2000, she brought people to their feet. In that moment, it was as if a bolt of lightning had cut through the gathering storm clouds of controversy and division plaguing the Christian church in recent years. She was clearing the air by calling attention to truly central concerns, beyond the liberal-versus-conservative

15

deadlocked battles that seemed to keep people arguing about the Bible instead of plumbing its depths. "Do not abandon the Bible to the Bible-bashers and the Bible-thumpers," she urged. "Reclaim the Bible. Do not let go of it until it blesses you."[2]

Professor Trible was speaking to preachers, whose job it is to wrestle with the Scriptures. I hope these words of mine will appeal to many thoughtful Christians—those who are questioning either a liberal or literalist past and are seeking to move into a deeper, more secure faith, and those who are seeking faith. Bible "thumpers" claim that the Bible comprises the exact words of God dictated to divinely chosen individuals, while the Bible "bashers" see it merely as the words of human writers. But thumpers and bashers both tend to look to the Bible for truth in "the facts"—the "what" rather than the "who." They treat the Bible only as an object of analysis and verification, rather than the way of God to us; God in person whose story it is, who speaks to us and comes to us in the Jesus of Nazareth whom we meet through this book.

The Bible is for *you*, not for the debates of critics and defenders. It is not the preserve of scholars. It is for everyone—man, woman, and child, priest or pew-warmer, religious or irreligious. The Bible is primarily intended to be read not for information, but for experiencing a relationship with God at ever-deepening levels.

Our Spiritual Hunger

We live in a time of intense social and cultural change, perhaps as great as any other transition in human history. Such intensive and extensive change results in great moral and ethical confusion combined with spiritual hunger. In the 1990s, "spirituality" became a buzzword. In the relative prosperity of the 1980s, many people sought satisfaction and security in accumulating material things, only to discover that they failed to bring lasting satisfaction. The next decade was marked by a search for deeper meaning in daily life: stable personal relationships, lasting and happy marriages, and satisfying personal and social values. At the start of a new millennium, our need to find meaning, value, and purpose in life continues to drive an intense interest in spirituality. Evidence of this abounds:

- Bestseller lists include books about mystical journeys of inner illumination, apocalyptic events in the so-called "end times," and self-help guides professing to offer spiritual counsel on every topic imaginable.

- Aboriginal peoples have rediscovered their "native spiritualities," which in turn have been adapted and popularized by non-native people.

- In the 1960s, numerous spiritual practices and disciplines of the East were discovered by the popular youth culture of the West. As a result, yoga, transcendental meditation, Tai Chi, Kung Fu, acupuncture, and Chinese medicine are more accepted today.

- So-called "New Age" spirituality seeks an underlying unity of both animate and inanimate things. Even in the field of physical science, there appear to be openings for the recognition of spiritual reality. The "Gaia theory" of James Lovelock and Lynn Margulis[3] suggests the earth is a living, self-regulating organism rather than just the "third rock from the sun." Lovelock, an atmospheric chemist, and Margulis (former wife of Carl Sagan), a microbiologist, have joined many other leading scientists who are recognizing that physical theories and empirical knowledge do not explain all that there is. The books of Paul Davies, John Polkinghorne, and others from a Christian perspective, and that of Fritjof Capra who deals with Eastern religions, seek to bridge the traditional gulf between science and religion.

Many people are searching, some desperately, for deeper meaning in their lives, a purpose worth living for, a reality beyond the material and the physical. But "spirituality" is a vague term. Some of the hunger is driven by a search for something more definitive and personal. Douglas Coupland wrote in his novel *Life After God*,

Now—here is my secret.
I tell it to you with an openness of heart that I doubt I shall ever achieve again, so I pray that you are in a quiet room as you hear these words. My secret is that I need God—that I am sick and can

no longer make it alone. I need God to help me give, because I no longer seem to be capable of giving; to help me be kind, as I no longer seem capable of kindness; to help me love, as I seem beyond being able to love.[4]

Many people are crying and yearning not just for spiritual experience, but for God.

But many are not turning to religion itself. "I'm quite spiritual, but I don't claim to be religious," they say. There is a vacuum, a sense of personal emptiness that seems unfulfilled by rituals or systems of belief. Such people seek a genuine encounter with God.

The Bible offers to lead us into the encounter with God for which we long, but the great riches of the Bible will elude us if we continue to marginalize it as an object for our investigation, to ascertain whether its facts are reliable and true. It is not simply the passive object of our imperious and supposedly impartial study. It does not yield its treasures to those who come to it with preconceived agendas. If we allow it to be the Word of God, the Bible questions us, challenges us, and forms our agendas.

The Bible Lost and Found

At one time, the Bible was a very important part of Western culture. Not only was it a significant public symbol used in civil ceremonies and courts of law, it was also in the heart and on the tongue of the average citizen. It provided comfort and hope to many people, who viewed it as the basis of their spirituality and the foundation of meaning and purpose for daily living. It was not unusual to come across people who claimed to have read it cover to cover not only once, but several times, and who could quote from it at length. Most children could recite Psalm 23, the Lord's Prayer, and often additional passages.

Through the twentieth century, the Bible seemed to be losing its power in society at large. Its authority was questioned, not just outside religious circles, but in churches as well. Preachers still quoted it, people sometimes argued about it, but in most homes it sat on a shelf gathering dust, no longer a part of everyday living. For most people, even for many Christians, the Bible seemed incomprehensible or simply irrelevant.

Recent years have seen a revived interest in the Bible as a source of spiritual nurture and a basis for living. As a significant influence in the development of much that is good in Western culture, some, in recent times, are wondering if they can find in the Bible that which gave meaning and comfort to earlier generations. The Bible can be a difficult book to understand, even for those who can recite chapters and verses from it. It has occasioned much confusion and conflict within the context of scientific advancement and biblical scholarship. Some are alienated by the ways in which the Bible is read and handled by those who take every word of it literally and use it to influence others. Others conclude that the Bible is simply a collection of unreliable, if fascinating, documents that either ignore or distort actual history. There is great contention over the Bible's place in classical literature and its origins in the history of religion. Today, even within many churches and programs of Christian spirituality, the Bible is often neglected. I recently attended an event in which the Bible was not even mentioned, even though the event was led by the pastor of a large congregation noted for its ministries in Christian spirituality.

The way we often treat the Bible is really a misuse of the Bible. New Testament scholar Walter Wink began his book *The Bible in Human Transformation*[5] with the sentence, "Historical biblical criticism is bankrupt." He was referring to the method of scholarly Bible study—the scientific study of the Bible as an object of history—that had occupied most Bible scholars since the rise of historical criticism in the eighteenth century. He didn't mean that this criticism had been worthless, "incapable of producing useful products," but that it was "no longer able to accomplish its avowed purpose."[6]

The scientific study of the Bible through historical criticism has been, in many ways, a great help in understanding the Bible. But such studies have tended to treat the Bible as an object for scientific scrutiny rather than a place to meet and hear God. In addition, historical criticism raised a violent reaction from people who believed it was not treating the Bible as the Word of God. It is significant that this defense of the Bible also used reason and scientific evidence as the basis of its critique. Both sought the "truth" in the facts, treating the Bible as an object to be examined rather than the basis of a relationship with God.

Entering the Bible on its own terms requires that we read it in a way that is radically different from the way we read most other books, and perhaps, radically different from what we have traditionally thought of as Bible reading. When we read the Bible for the facts alone, our hearts tend to be deadened to the Word of God. When we read it for the who instead of the what, we may begin to take on a bit of the radiance of the love of God.

Can we understand the Bible in a way that helps us to make it central to our living, that gives us a relationship with the One whose Word it is rather than just giving us certain historical facts that seem to have little relevance to our life today? Can the Bible become again a more central authority in the life of the church, the recognized basis of Christian spirituality? In what twentieth-century theologian Karl Barth calls the "strange new world within the Bible,"[7] we can find a relationship with One who is calling us in grace and love and seeking from us a response in faith. This way of understanding and appreciating the Bible doesn't deny scientific knowledge or require diluting the power and truth of the Word of God. The Bible is an invitation to a relationship with God and with others. Beyond the thumpers and the bashers, the Bible can come alive personally in a fresh, new way if we make it once again basic to our living, reading the Bible not for the facts but for the love of God.

This is not some new spiritual discipline, another task for Christians in an already busy life. It is not a call to return to the old chapter-a-day method of reading the Bible, to be followed mechanically if diligently. The necessity is to make the Bible once again basic to every aspect of our life. In this era where life is so busy and time so scarce, each of us must find our own methods and develop our own habits to include the Bible in our lives. Further, I believe that participating in a community of faith and being attentive to the reading and exposition of the Word week by week is essential for making the Bible again central to our living.

Why is the "who" of the Bible so important? The answer is that there is a particular quality of life that comes from a trusting, loving relationship with God, a relationship that is nurtured in God's Word.

My Search for God

My own search for God began with a restlessness of soul and led gradually to a deepening encounter with God in the Bible. Twenty-one years old, with university behind me, I had quit a promising career in the financial world. I realized that I had only one life to live and I knew I didn't want to spend it working in a bank. I began working in a steel plant in general labor and was wondering what to do with the rest of my life. I was looking for "my vocation," a purpose for my life. It was a time of intense spiritual searching.

One lovely summer day, the sun warm and the shade of the trees pleasant, I walked slowly in a public park under the shade of the trees, by a pond where the ducks were chortling quietly to themselves. Though I couldn't say I really believed in God, I knew there was something missing in my life. Deep down I knew I was faced with a Reality greater than the things for which most people seemed to be striving.

Though there were many people there that Sunday afternoon, one man sat apart by himself. Without knowing quite why, only that it seemed something I must do, I went up to him and asked him to pray for me. This took some courage, since it's not something I usually do. In fact, never before or since have I gone up to a stranger and asked for prayer. It was an act of desperation. I've always been grateful to that man in the park, though I never knew his name and never saw him again. I'm sure that he did pray for me, as he said he would.

When I did "find God" it seemed rather that God had found me. It wasn't any sensational "born again" experience with God speaking to me out of a bush or cloud, there were no flashes of lightning nor voices in the night. It took a couple of years of intense searching, but gradually, very gradually, God became wonderfully real. I began to understand that the main purpose of my life and ministry was to help people find faith. That early meeting in the park was one part of a long process, but it was significant. In the decades since then, through years of life— marriage and children, ministry in churches large and small— helping others find faith has come to me as the central thing I was to be about. I believe that God was working that day in that strange incident.

I remember one day, early in my search, when I first realized the magnitude of faith. I was in church one Sunday as was my custom, even though God was still a pretty remote proposition. The readings that day included Psalm 46, beginning with these verses:

God is our refuge and strength, a very present help in trouble. Therefore we will not fear, though the earth should change, though the mountains shake in the heart of the sea . . . . The Lord of hosts is with us; the God of Jacob is our refuge.

It suddenly occurred to me, with considerable force, that we have neither refuge nor final security other than God. In an atomic age, when "the windows of heaven are opened, and the foundations of the earth tremble, . . . the earth is utterly broken, the earth is torn asunder, the earth is violently shaken. The earth staggers like a drunkard" (Isaiah 24:18–20), there can be no security nor salvation other than in the One who created the heavens and the earth.

At that time I was working in the Royal Bank of Canada. One of our customers had been an officer in the Canadian armed services during World War II. Although he now worked in a warehouse, he liked to live his former officer's lifestyle on a low-wage income. He would come into the bank all smiles, joking with members of the staff, but all the while watching the door of the credit manager's office. When he saw the door open, his face would change as his smile fell away, replaced by a haggard anxiety as he walked through the door and tried to work out some way of maintaining his credit and paying his debts.

Older women, well made-up and coiffed, dressed in fine though slightly faded and out-of-date clothing, also spent much time in that same office trying to find a way of maintaining their extravagant lifestyles with dwindling finances.

I began to realize how much we overvalue money, how impossibly we look for ultimate security in mammon. Experiences such as these drove me to leave a budding financial career and embark upon a life of discovering the God who is revealed to us in the Bible. In the years since, I have wrestled with God, rejoiced in his grace, and ministered to people in joy and sorrow, marriage and divorce, in illness and despair, and in birth and death. Through it all, I have tried to help them find and develop faith—a relationship with and a trust and confidence in the One we may come to know through the book we call the Word of God. I haven't regretted it (at least not for a day or two at a time). In the following pages, I look forward to sharing with you answers to your questions of finding and nurturing faith and to helping in your struggles to understand God's ways. In the process, I hope your own spiritual hunger will be increased as well as satisfied by seeing the Bible as a richly rewarding invitation to know God in a personal sense. Whatever problems you have had or may continue to have with the Bible, I hope that what is here may help you to find faith if you're looking or to strengthen the faith that may already have found you.

2

CHANGING TIMES, CHANGING VIEWS

Amid New Understanding, a Place for the Personal

We operate as though the machine manufactures the reality. . . .
Even our own minds and bodies we most often describe nowadays
in terms of mechanisms, ignoring their organic, pond-like nature.
But if we are to assimilate this new information about the world,
the machine will have to be junked. There is something more here
than it can measure. What that is all but baffles our imagination.
"God knows," even physicists are tempted to say, throwing up
their hands. Exactly.

Virginia Stem Owens[1]

C ulture," said the archbishop, "is the way we do things
around here."[2] Culture is the context in which we live,
expressed not only in the arts and literature but also in the
folkways, aphorisms, and assumptions of society. Culture is what
emerges from the worldview of a particular society, the way a
society sees and understands its existence in the world around it.

Two of the major formative influences in Western culture over
the last five hundred years—modern science and the Bible—have
coexisted in tension. To appreciate and understand the Bible in
terms of a relationship with God, we need a cultural worldview

that affirms the importance of the personal dimension in understanding reality and shaping human experience. The increasing influence of scientific understanding in the last several hundred years has tended to marginalize the personal, leading to a struggle for what Wolfgang Kohler called "the place of value in a world of facts."[3] This influence has distorted our understanding of the Bible, making it difficult to understand the Bible in relational terms. However, because of crucial developments in the sciences, there seems to be an increasing recognition of the reality of the spiritual and a place for the personal.

The scientific endeavors of the past three hundred years have yielded spectacular discoveries in medicine, electronics, transportation, communication, and virtually every sphere of human activity. Not many of us would deny ourselves the benefits of up-to-date medical treatment, labor-saving devices, telephone or television, or the computer. Yet the sheer scope of scientific advances has led us to overestimate the power of science. Science, by its very nature, is not able to tell us the meaning and purpose of life. Therefore, we have relegated such issues to the realm of individual opinion and subjective experience, beyond objective verification. The result, as British missionary and statesman Lesslie Newbigin has noted, is a dichotomy in our culture between public truth (the world of facts) and personal opinion (the world of values).

After forty years as a Christian missionary in India, Newbigin returned to England to find churches there in severe decline. He began asking why the only places where the Christian church was not vital and growing were in so-called "Christian countries." This eventually led to his book, *Foolishness to the Greeks: The Gospel and Modern Culture,*[4] and to a movement in England and North America commonly known as "The Gospel and Contemporary Culture." Newbigin's work argued for the distinctiveness of the gospel amid the assumptions of Western culture.

Although much in twentieth-century physical science has moved beyond these assumptions, they are still common in popular understanding. Following are three of the most foundational:

- Empiricism, which insists that all knowledge is based on observation, experimentation, and verification, has led to belief in a self-sufficient universe that can be understood and explained on its own terms, without the need for any reference to the transcendent or to God. As Newbigin observed, "The most obvious fact that distinguishes our culture from all that have preceded it is that it is—in its public philosophy at least—atheist. The famous reply of Laplace to the complaint that he had omitted God from his system—'I have no need of that hypothesis'—might stand as a motto for our culture as a whole."[5]

- The belief in natural causation, the law of cause and effect, has led to determinism, which in turn has led to an understanding of reality as mechanical, including the ways in which we view the origin of life and the nature of our humanity.

- Emphasis on analysis (observation and experimentation) has led to increased specialization (reductionism). This has resulted in the loss of a sense of purpose and any place for value. You can take a machine apart to see how it works, but you have to put it back together to understand its purpose and put it to use. Specialization has resulted in many wonderful discoveries, but it cannot unite discrete parts into a meaningful whole. Newbigin used the concept of a "pattern" to explain the limitations of the assumptions inherent in scientific analysis:

While we attend to the pattern we are only subsidiarily aware of the details. But a complete account of the details by itself would not enable us to recognize a pattern. . . . Our recognition of a significant pattern is an act of personal judgment for which there are no rules. It is a judgment of value: the pattern represents something a human being finds meaningful in terms of intrinsic beauty or of purpose.[6]

This modern worldview has been so pervasive that it was only in the closing years of the twentieth century that we began to recognize these assumptions and to see a breakdown in the confidence that science and technology (the techniques and tools which result from scientific endeavor) will provide solutions to all our problems, social and personal, as well as scientific and technological. We are growing increasingly aware, in our popular understanding, that there are dimensions of human experience and knowledge that cannot be explained by the scientific method.

For instance, the human capacity for self-transcendence (self-consciousness) means that there are dimensions of our humanity that cannot be understood by science. A person is more than the sum of the parts. Augustine, in his meditation on memory in *The Confessions*, pointed out that our memory intimates our capacity to transcend time, to stand outside of time and to remember the past. Similarly, we are able to be conscious of ourselves within a certain place. This capacity to be conscious of ourselves within time and space indicates an ability to transcend time and space. Therefore we cannot understand ourselves in purely empirical terms.

As Newtonian science seeks to operate in purely empirical terms, it has difficulty in finding a place for the personal. In the new worldview emerging at the beginning of this new millennium, there must be a place for the personal.

From the Mechanical to the Personal

Over a century ago, Matthew Arnold wrote with amazing foresight that we are "wandering between two worlds, one dead, the other powerless to be born."[7] Today, that old world—the modern era—is not dead, but it is obviously dying, and the new world, while not yet born, is certainly laboring and struggling for birth.

At the beginning of the twenty-first century, we seem to be living in an in-between age. We call the era striving to be born the postmodern era. We are now beginning to recognize the limitations of the assumptions of the modern era. Although it has given us marvelous insights into the mechanical workings of our universe, it could not comprehend anything beyond the mechanical and the empirical. Therefore, the personal and the transcendent were beyond its comprehension. As literary critic Northrop Frye observed

> The world of nature [is] the world within which our physical bodies have evolved, but from which consciousness feels oddly separated. . . . The systematic study of nature, which is the main business of science, reflects this sense of separation. It is impersonal,

avoids value judgments and commitments to emotion or imagination, and confines itself to explanations that are largely in terms
of mechanism.[8]

The modern era remains the primary context for our current
ways of reading and understanding the Bible. Once we understand this historical backdrop, it becomes clear why we have tried
so desperately to understand the Bible in terms of the truth of its
facts rather than seeing it as an invitation to a personal relationship with God, a place of encounter with the Eternal.

Now, in the so-called postmodern era, we are beginning to see
the world in a new way, which allows a place for the spiritual and
the personal at the core of our understanding of reality. If energy
and matter are interchangeable, if the chair on which I sit is a
form of energy, a concatenation of atoms, is this a physical or a
spiritual universe? Science will say that if it is measurable, it is
physical. Yet what is there, really? The atom (from the Greek *ato-
mos*, meaning "indivisible"), once defined as the smallest indivisible measurement of matter, has been split and split again, until
we now see it as mostly empty space. Fritjof Capra observes,

> There are no particles in atoms, such as the balls in the atomic
> model. There are no hard and solid spheres or objects like grains
> of sand. A sub-atomic particle is essentially a set of relationships
> reaching outward to other things, and the other things are again
> relationships to yet other things.[9]

Relativity and Relationship

The development of the physical sciences through the twentieth century began to focus more upon relationships and interac-
tions than upon discrete objects.[10] Einstein's theories of Special
and General Relativity say in part that what we see is relative to
our position or perspective. To say that all knowledge is relative
may not be so far from saying that all knowledge is relational.

To say that all knowledge is relative is not to say that there are
no absolutes, but only to accept that we do not have absolute
knowledge of the absolutes. We are not infallible, collectively or
individually. In fact, "relativism" is often defined as the belief that

all knowledge is relational. "Relative" means either (1) someone to whom you are related (usually by blood or marriage), (2) an implied comparison, or (3) grammatically, a "relative pronoun." To "relate" is to recount an experience or tell a story. This is one way we tie things together to make sense of them, to find in them a meaningful pattern.

Twentieth-century scientist and philosopher Michael Polanyi has proposed that all knowledge is properly understood as "personal knowledge." The implications of his thought push relativity onto the personal level. His book *Personal Knowledge: Towards a Post-Critical Philosophy*, published in the 1950s, claimed that the "knower"—the scientist, philosopher, or you or me—is personally involved in all acts of understanding and rejected the idea that the observer can be completely objective, impersonal and detached:

> I start by rejecting the ideal of scientific detachment. In the exact sciences, this false ideal is perhaps harmless, for it is in fact disregarded there by scientists. But we shall see that it exercises a destructive influence in biology, psychology and sociology, and falsifies our whole outlook far beyond the domain of science. I want to establish an alternative ideal of knowledge . . . the personal participation of the knower in all acts of understanding.[11]

Polanyi emphasized the importance of what he called "tacit knowledge." Take, for instance, learning to write with a pen or pencil. At first it's a slow, laborious process as our hand and fingers attempt to guide the pencil and form the letters. Later, the pencil will become a kind of extension of our hand, so much a part of the operation that we become quite unconscious of it. Polanyi used the illustration of a radiologist who must learn to read x-rays, seeing beyond vague shadows of black, white, and grey to forms that others cannot see.

When we stop to consider it, a great part of our knowing and doing is by means of tacit knowledge. Most expressions of human craft or artistic endeavor operate largely with tacit knowledge. The way we see and understand our world depends in large part on such knowledge—what we have been taught to see and understand. From our infancy, we have acquired ways of seeing things, of understanding our world and its workings that we have learned within our particular tradition and culture. We see our world today according to the concepts of natural law developed in the last five hundred years of the modern era. The sun, moon, and planets move in accordance with natural law. The life of the earth around us operates by natural law. Even Western medical understanding of the human body is largely limited to its functioning according to laws of cause and effect.

We live in a period of turbulent change and it may be many years before a new worldview becomes clear. But it does appear that the development of the physical sciences through the twentieth century, along with the recognition of the limits of scientific endeavor, may help us to realize again the importance of the relational and the personal.[12] Already we can see the possibility that this emerging understanding is more favorable to viewing the Bible in personal and relational terms. Perhaps future generations will more easily understand and appreciate the message of the Bible than readers of this past century.

3

BEYOND THE BIBLE
BATTLES

Understanding the Bible in Relational Terms

> We have all been troubled with the thought that there are so many kinds of Christianity in the world . . . all of them appealing with the same earnestness and zeal to the Bible. Each insists, *Ours* is the religion revealed in the Bible, or at least its most legitimate successor. And how is one to answer? . . . "Yea, let God be true, but every man a liar."
>
> Karl Barth[1]

The responses of the various Christian traditions to scientific advances have been quite ambivalent. Faith has existed in uneasy tension with science since Galileo. Up until the triumph of reason over revelation in the early years of the modern era leading up to the Enlightenment, theology was often termed "the queen of the sciences." Since the Enlightenment, theology, along with biblical scholarship, has often allowed itself to become the handmaid of the sciences. On the other hand, theology has attempted to reject the encroachment of science into areas of revelation, asserting the truth of Christian doctrine and the Bible over the new knowledge, which science seemed to be providing.

Through the years of the twentieth century, the Protestant/ Evangelical[2] churches were split over the question of the relation of science and religion, especially in regard to our understanding of the Bible. As science increased its influence, the power and influence of the churches of Western culture has dimmed to the point that it seems almost extinct. Since the time of the Roman emperor Constantine in the fourth century, Christianity has been recognized, formally or informally, as the established religion of Western culture. The church was a power sometimes equal to the state. Christendom, as it was called, seems to be at an end—at least for the foreseeable future. Religion has been overpowered by the scientific endeavor.

Some in the churches sought to reconcile the Bible—its account of creation, the history of the Hebrew people, and the stories of the life of Jesus, especially the miracles, with scientific understanding. Others, in the face of the seeming certainty of scientific knowledge, continued to assert the factual, literal truth of the biblical accounts. Both treated the Bible as a modern history or science book and demanded either skepticism toward or acceptance of the "facts as presented in the Bible."

Modernism Versus Fundamentalism

On a Sunday in May 1922, Harry Emerson Fosdick, a Baptist minister in the pulpit of New York City's First Presbyterian Church, preached a sermon titled, "Shall the Fundamentalists Win?"

For a number of years a storm had been brewing. In 1909, Charles Eliot, a professor emeritus at Harvard University, gave a widely reported lecture on "The Future of Religion" in which he advocated a kind of religious humanism based on love of God and neighbor, and devoid of churches, Scriptures, and formal liturgy and worship. In response, Presbyterian Princeton issued five dogmas that were published just before World War I as a series of twelve volumes entitled, *The Fundamentals: A Testimony to the Truth*. They affirmed that fundamental to Christian faith were certain beliefs: the virgin birth of Jesus, the inerrancy of the Bible, the physical resurrection, the substitutionary understanding of the atonement, and the imminent, physical second coming of Christ. After the war these booklets were given wide circulation by two wealthy laymen.[3]

"Fundamentalism," as it came to be called, arose as a protest against the tendency in Protestant theology to accommodate Christian doctrine and biblical understanding to contemporary scientific knowledge. The study of the Bible was subjected to methods of scientific study and historical criticism that, for all its subsequent benefits, sometimes left little of the Bible intact and often grossly exceeded its claim to scientific truth and objectivity.

> In the nineteenth and twentieth centuries, critics laid great emphasis on the presumed objectivity of their studies. They tried to place biblical criticism among the sciences. But a cursory examination of the "assured results" of their investigations will show that they exaggerated their own objectivity.[4]

Many theologians, pastors, and laypeople felt as if the very foundations of the Christian faith were under attack. The controversy grew exceedingly grim. A Presbyterian layman, head of a New York publicity organization, gave Fosdick's sermon wide circulation under the title, "The New Knowledge and the Christian Faith." The storm broke in full fury.

As a good liberal, Fosdick claimed that his sermon was "a plea for tolerance."

> I stated the honest differences of conviction dividing these two groups, . . . and then made my plea that the desirable solution was not a split that would tear the evangelical church asunder, but a spirit of conciliation that would work out the problem within an inclusive fellowship.[5]

However, the title of the sermon and some of the content indicated a bias against "the reactionary group," as Fosdick sharply critiqued the fundamentalists for "one of the worst exhibitions of bitter intolerance that the churches of this country have ever seen."[6] Instead of a plea for tolerance, Fosdick's sermon was seen as a declaration of war.

In 1925, during a scorching month of July, one of the fiercest public battles of this war occurred in Dayton, Tennessee. It was one of the most publicized legal cases of the century. John Thomas Scopes, a local science teacher, was charged with violating a Tennessee state law prohibiting the teaching of the theory of evolution in public schools. The law stated that it was "unlawful for any teacher in any of the universities, normals, and all other public schools of the state, to teach any theory that denies the story of the divine creation of man as taught in the Bible, and to teach instead that man had descended from a lower order of animals."

"The Scopes Monkey Trial" became a public sensation. It pitted the famous orator William Jennings Bryan, advocate of Fundamentalism and three-time unsuccessful candidate for the United States presidency, against Clarence S. Darrow, the most famous criminal lawyer of that generation. The newspapers covered the case extensively—each day of the trial some 175,000 words were telegraphed out of Dayton to newspapers across the United States, and even to Europe, as millions of people followed the case. In 1955 the play *Inherit the Wind,* a fictional dramatization of the event, ran on Broadway in New York City and was later made into a movie.[7]

The battle over the Bible continues to the present time. The lines of the divide are not as firm as in the early decades of the past century. The public has become somewhat bored with the ongoing struggle, but division still exists and the continuing debate between Creationists and Evolutionists indicates that there is still not only division, but also real antagonism. In 1999, the Kansas Board of Education voted to remove the teaching of evolution from the school curriculum throughout their midwestern state, a decision that has since been rescinded.

The tragedy is that the whole dispute is irrelevant! The Bible is neither a science book nor a history book, but something else entirely. It is the Word of God, which has been widely misunderstood and misinterpreted because of such unnecessary and irrelevant quarrelling. People who are searching desperately for spiritual reality and personal meaning are sadly deprived of what is basic to Christian living and of what has given rise to so much that is good in Western culture and heritage.

Between a scientific worldview that seems to leave no place for God and a biblical spirituality that has lost its roots, it's not an easy time for the Christian faith. Many people dismiss the Christian faith without even trying it out. To some, even belief in God doesn't make any sense, and this is true of some of the smartest and best among us. Others make an attempt at faith, but when what they find doesn't satisfy their experience, they turn away. What is the basis of our faith? Can we find again and reconnect with the roots of our Christian spirituality?

Pastor and scholar Eugene Peterson has helped many to rediscover these roots. Through his writings and his translation of the Bible, *The Message,*[8] Peterson points us back beyond the Reformers, the church fathers, and the ascetics of the fourth century to the Bible as the Word of God.

True reformers often are the ones who lead us on by taking us back. True radicals show us the roots (from the Latin *radix,* the root of our word "radical") from which we are nurtured. It was Elton Trueblood in the mid-twentieth century who spoke of Western culture as a "cut-flower culture"—cut off from its roots, wilting and dying in reality even while it seems to continue to flourish. Radicals such as Peterson help us rediscover our roots in order to find the source of our life.

Peterson calls for us to return to "Square One," to the basis of Christian faith and life in the Word of God.

The Christian life consists in what God does for us, not what we do for God . . . the Christian life consists in what God says to us, not what we say about God. We also, of course, do things and say things, but if we do not return to Square One each time we act, each time we speak, beginning from God and God's Word, we will soon be found to be practicing a spirituality that has little to do or nothing to do with God.

And so it is necessary, if we are going to truly live a Christian life, and not just use the word Christian to disguise our narcissistic and promethean attempts at a spirituality without worshipping God and without being addressed by God, it is necessary to return to Square One and adore God and listen to God. Given our sin-damaged memories that render us vulnerable to every latest edition of journalistic spirituality, daily re-orientation in the truth revealed in Jesus and attested in Scripture is required. And given our ancient predisposition for reducing every scrap of divine revelation that we come across into a piece of moral/spiritual technology that we can use to get on in the world, and eventually to get on with God, a daily return to a condition of not-knowing and non-achievement is required. We have proven, time and again, that we are not to be trusted in these matters. We need to return to Square One for a fresh start as often as every morning, noon, and night.[9]

The Bible on Its Own Terms

To the diligent reader, the Bible reveals wonderful surprises. We have a tremendous challenge and a wonderful opportunity. The Bible still speaks. The Word of God still holds its gracious power. But we must approach it on its own terms and understand it, not first of all as science or history, or the "facts," but in relational terms, calling us to intimacy with the One who not only created us, but continues to reach out to us in love. The Bible is first of all about relationships—our relationship with God and our relationship with one another.

In addition to the influence of science and modernity, our understanding of the Bible has been greatly shaped by the Greek, classical tradition. In Greek ontology, the understanding of "being" tends to be static, whereas the Hebrew view is more dynamic. When Moses asks God (Yahweh) for his name, the enigmatic reply is usually translated "I am that (or what or who) I am!" (Exodus 3:14). It can also be translated more dynamically, "I will be what (or who) I will be." The influence of Greek thought has resulted in an emphasis on propositions and dogmas, what we believe rather than in whom we believe.

In biblical understanding, "knowing" has as much to do with personal relationships as with factual knowledge. "Now the man knew his wife Eve, and she conceived" (Genesis 4:1). Again, in the New Testament, "[Joseph} knew her not until she had borne a son" (Matthew 1:25 RSV). The very phrase "the Word of God" implies address and hearing, involving personal terms of call and response, God's call to us implying our "response-ability," rather than the mechanistic reaction of "cause and effect"— "I and thou," rather than "it and me." In Martin Buber's terms:

One cannot divide one's life between an actual relationship with God and an inactual I-it relationship to the world. Whoever knows the world as something to be utilized knows God the same way.[10]

The phrase "the truth will make you free" (John 8:32), which stands over the gates of many a university, is commonly understood in the classical sense, referring to intellectual truth and a knowledge of objective facts. In its New Testament sense, it should be understood in a relational sense, as for example, being true to a spouse or friend. Notice that the passage goes on to speak of being slaves of sin and says, "If the Son makes you free, you will be free indeed" (John 8:36). Belief merely in propositions, dogmas, or facts is not going to make us free of sin.

In Genesis 1, we read that humanity was created in the image of God: "So God created humankind in his image, in the image of God he created them" (Genesis 1:27). Scholars and theologians from the earliest days have wrestled with this phrase, the "image of God." The "image" should be understood, I suggest, not as something in us, a spark of divinity called a soul, independent of God, but as humanity created for responsible relationship with God, humanity able to respond to God. We are "response-able," able to respond to God and to others. We find fulfillment in life chiefly in relationships with one another, in *agape* love, and ultimately, in relationship with God.

Righteousness, in the New Testament sense, is not the self-righteousness that results from keeping the law, but a right relationship with God and with others through *agape*, Christian love. The sad fact, of course, is that we are not fully responsible. Our relationships with others are often fractured and broken, and we find ourselves lonely and afraid, longing for relationship. In the story of Adam and Eve, the advent of sin leads to the corruption of our relationship with God, with one another, and with the good earth that supports us.

Our relationships are compromised by our self-centeredness. Because we have sought to "be like God" (Genesis 3:5), to put ourselves at the center of life where only God must be, we feel estranged. We do not have the communion with God or the loving relationships with others we were created to enjoy. This results in our sense of wrong, of guilt, of essential estrangement—our sin.

Sin is anything that breaks these relationships—an offense against God because it hurts and harms God's children or God's creation. Sin happens when our concern for ourselves—our own happiness, our own security—thwarts our ability to reach out to

God and to others. Sin is not trivial; it is deadly serious. When it breaks our relationship with God, we no longer know God, and therefore we no longer understand who we truly are or why we are here. Without awareness of life's meaning and purpose, in the truest sense we are "lost."

One response is to make rules and rituals which, when we keep them, give us some release from feelings of failure and guilt. But the trouble with rules and rituals is that they are one-sided. They may be helpful, but they are not essential to the relationship, and in fact, if rigidly adhered to, may impede the relationship.

In the time of Jesus, one group of people, the Pharisees, was quite fastidious about keeping the law of God as revealed in the Old Testament. They kept every i dotted and t crossed, every "jot and tittle" (Matthew 5:18 KJV). They were neither stupid nor wicked, but were in many ways fine, moral, "good" people. But Jesus saw the fallacy in their righteousness. It was self-righteousness. They were so concerned with their own religious performance that they could not enter wholeheartedly into a relationship with others, especially those who were morally or ritually inferior. Their very goodness became an obstacle to real goodness, to mercy and grace, and their righteousness a block in any relationship. So Jesus said to his disciples, "Unless your righteousness exceeds that of the scribes and Pharisees, you will never enter the kingdom of heaven" (Matthew 5:20).

Jesus went on immediately in what we call "the Sermon on the Mount" (Matthew 5–7) to interpret the law and the Ten Commandments in such a way that no one can claim to be righteous before God. "You have heard that it was said to those of ancient times, 'You shall not murder'. . . But I say to you that if you are angry with a brother or sister, you will be liable to judgment. . . . You have heard that it was said, 'You shall not commit adultery.' But I say to you that everyone who looks at a woman with lust has already committed adultery with her in his heart" (Matthew 5:21–28). Our relationship depends first of all upon God's grace and mercy, not our own righteousness.

When the Pharisees tried to test Jesus, he told them that the law and the prophets could be summed up in two commands— to love God and to love one's neighbor. Our lives can be fulfilled only in relationship with God and with one another.

Faith is first of all a matter, not of belief in certain dogmas or facts, but of a relationship with God-in-Christ. It is a matter of trust in God's grace and mercy. It is not so much about what we believe but in whom we place our trust. It is possible because we know God's love and grace in the life and death of Jesus Christ. Repentance is not a turning from sin, which we are really not able to do in our own strength; it is a returning to the relationship that has been broken.

One of the most grievous facets of our modern worldview is our attempt to understand personal relationships in mechanical terms, including our relationship with God. Some prayer groups seem "wired." As soon as one person sits down, another jumps up. Those who claim Jesus as "my personal Savior" sometimes seem to see the relationship as mechanical rather than personal.

Salvation itself is often understood as this kind of mechanical transaction—if we repent and are sufficiently sorry for our sin, then God will relent and forgive us. Charles Grandison Finney, the great revivalist of the nineteenth century in the United States, developed what he called "methods"—techniques to insure that people had a proper salvation experience. Unfortunately, evangelism in our own time sometimes still retains a too-great reliance upon techniques to ensure that as many as possible respond to the altar call.

Words seek to communicate, to relate. God, through his Word, seeks a relationship with us. God's Word calls for a response in order for communion to take place. Although we are able to respond to God's Word and, by the grace of God, to enter into a relationship with God and "walk by faith," we are also free to not choose this relationship and to continue to walk alone without the knowledge and the confidence of the love of God.

I believe that this appeal to understand the Bible in terms of a relationship rather than as facts is not a departure from the truth, but rather a return to an understanding of the Bible on its own terms. May it disarm our battles, inducing us to turn our doctrinal swords into ploughshares for working the rich soil of the Word of God.

4

FINDING A BASIS
FOR FAITH

The Bible and
the Word of God

"You search the scriptures because you think that in them you
have eternal life; and it is they that testify on my behalf."

John 5:39

The Bible invites us into a relationship with God, and faith
is the means by which we enter into this relationship. But
the word "faith" has been used and abused in such varied
ways that it has become troublesome and confusing for many people. Some assume faith is reserved only for those who have the
capacity to believe. Others see it as an act of religious willpower—
as the little boy in Sunday school defined it, "faith is how you
believe what you don't think is true." Still others dismiss it as a
psychological crutch or an irrational loyalty to a particular religious system, inclining to dangerous fanaticism.

"Christian faith" can mean very different things to different
people depending on how the Bible is read and understood. Which

parts of the Bible are the most important for informing our faith? What is intended to be normative for Christians everywhere, and what is no longer applicable due to changing times and cultures? These are endlessly vexing questions if we relegate faith simply to facts and dogmas. But if we look at faith as a dimension of divine relationship, we can see more clearly how the Bible shapes and nurtures it.

Pastors are often assumed to be superlative role models of faith, at least by those who don't know them intimately. I don't claim to be an especially spiritual person—probably more practical than spiritual. But over the years I've developed a faith that I cherish, and I seem to have the ability to help people who are searching for faith in God, especially thoughtful questioners.

In my own search for the basis of faith, I questioned most of the traditions, practices, and beliefs of the Christian church. What came out was a faith of my own—what the apostle Paul called "my Gospel" (Romans 2:16). It has its own quirks, but it's mine. I think it's fairly orthodox—if orthodoxy is treated as an ideal rather than an idol.

"Orthodoxy" originally meant "right belief," literally, "correct" praise or worship. My dictionary defines it as "holding the correct or the currently accepted opinions especially on religious doctrine, not heretical or independent-minded; . . . in theology, in harmony with what is authoritatively approved." The monastic virtues were chastity, poverty, and obedience. Obedience meant not only right behavior, but also right belief—obedience to the accepted beliefs and doctrines of the church at the time. A heretic was one who "chose" what he believed, who held his own opinions. So orthodoxy is important, but it should not be a straitjacket. As soon as we dictate what it is, as soon as we define it closely, it seems to dissipate. In the best sense we don't define it— orthodoxy defines us.

It is vital that faith respect and cherish orthodoxy, but faith is personal. It cannot be second-hand, a simple acceptance of what we are taught. Each of us must work out our own salvation, struggle with the ultimate questions of life, and embark on a personal search for God, remembering that "it is God who is at work in you enabling you both to will and to work for his good pleasure" (Philippians 2:12–13). But if faith is personal, then what is the basis for it?

Foundations of Faith

The "Wesleyan Quadrilateral"[1] cites four bases of Christian faith: reason, experience, tradition, and the Bible. In Protestantism, the Bible has been considered the primary source and basis of the Christian faith, in contrast to the emphasis in Catholicism upon papal authority and church teachings, and the emphasis in Eastern Orthodox tradition upon the ancient creeds and the wisdom of the church fathers.

Protestants claim the Bible alone as the only authority for faith, yet history illustrates the difficulty of gaining consensus among believers in defining the authority of the Bible as it relates to church and individual practice and the relationships between church and civil authorities. Therefore, Christians have sought the basis of faith in other foundations alongside the Bible such as tradition, spiritual experience, and human reason. Together, these four categories represent how Christians, to varying degrees emphasizing one over the others, construct a foundation for personal faith and corporate practice.

Tradition—the Witness of the Church: Some people would say they base their faith on the teaching of the church, the witness of the community of faith. After all, many very intelligent people have been struggling with these questions for hundreds of years. There have been thousands of books written by some of the best minds and hearts of human history. There is "a tradition." Surely we find the basis of our faith in that tradition whose accuracy and truth are ensured by the church. This tends to be the authority, the basis of belief, in the Catholic traditions, finding its most complete expression in the Roman tradition with its dogma of the "infallibility of the pope" speaking *ex cathedra.*

Tradition provides an external, objective authority for faith, but it is often an imposed rather than an owned or personal faith. Especially in the Western or Roman tradition, the emphasis has been on dogma—faith as what we believe rather than in whom we believe. For all the strength of tradition, the dynamism of the biblical revelation tends to get lost.

Experience—the Witness of the Holy Spirit: Many would say that we believe in God because of our own special experience of God. We associate the witness of the Spirit with a particular "religious experience," such as being born again. A familiar hymn affirms, "You ask me how I know He lives? He lives within my heart!"

In a day when any basis of faith is attacked on all sides, personal experience seems to be the reality that is unassailable—the reality of our own inner experience that no one else can finally deny. Such a basis for faith is personal, and much of the life and worship of Protestant churches has rightly emphasized faith as a personal response to the grace of God.

However, such an experiential basis of belief is highly individualistic. Those who make it the basis of their faith lack any objective basis or any corrective to subjective error. Often these persons tend to belong to the more "sectarian" branches of the church, and these are historically prone to division.

William James, in *The Varieties of Religious Experience* (his Gifford Lectures of 1902), while seeking to validate the reality of religious experience overall, questioned particular or subjective religious experience. He indicated that a "conversion experience" could be as valid and powerful from faith to atheism as it could from nonfaith to faith. James's work questioned subjective religious experience as a basis of faith. In spite of this, at the popular level of understanding, subjective experience is still commonly presented in some evangelical circles as the primary basis of our faith.

Reason—an Evaluation of Evidence and Experience: Some Christians point beyond particular spiritual experiences to their reflection upon the totality of their experience. Belief in God and in Jesus as the Christ seem reasonable to them in the light of their total knowledge and experience.

Some point to the world around them and say, "Of course there's a God! How do you explain the world if there is no God?" (as if the existence of God depended on their ok). These people reflect upon their experience of life, their knowledge of nature or of science and they conclude that belief in God is "reasonable." They look at the evidence of Jesus' resurrection in Scripture and in the history of the church and conclude that the belief that Jesus rose from the dead is the reasonable conclusion.

We don't always associate the work of the Spirit of God with the workings of our mind. But if the Spirit of God is the Spirit of truth, should not the existence of God and the reality of the life of Christ appear reasonable to us in light of the evidence? Should not the working of the Spirit of God in our hearts and lives be reasonable, as well as emotionally fulfilling?

Yet, while belief in God may be reasonable, reason does not bring us to a personal relationship with God. To paraphrase Luther, one may possess an appreciation of reason through Christ, but one cannot come to knowledge of Christ through reason. As reliance on "experience" may give us a religion of the heart exclusive of the mind, the reliance upon reason will leave us with a religion of the mind lacking the heart.

The Bible—the Witness of the Word: Perhaps few of us today would immediately think to say that we believe in God or trust in Christ because of the Bible, claiming the Bible is the basic authority of our faith. We've almost forgotten the seemingly simplistic reasoning of the Sunday school hymn of years ago, "Jesus loves me, this I know, For the Bible tells me so." Yet when theologian Karl Barth, who wrote the six-million-word, multivolume *Church Dogmatics,* was asked to sum up the gospel, these simple words were his only reply. This ditty from childhood days reveals the Bible as the traditional basis of faith of the Protestant tradition. The Bible was the authority on which the Reformer Martin Luther took his stand against the pope and the Roman church of his day. Central to our faith, in the various traditions emanating from the Protestant Reformation of the sixteenth century, is this collection of books we call the Bible.

But the authority of Scripture has become a problem in the church in the modern era. Critics point out that individualistic interpretations of Scripture have resulted in a vast array of Protestant churches, each with its particular understanding. The priesthood of all believers has been understood as the priesthood of each believer. The result is that, even in churches of the Protestant or evangelical tradition, many members would point to nature or to reason or to a personal, subjective experience rather than to the Bible as the basis of their belief in God and their faith in Jesus Christ.

These four bases of Christian faith—the tradition and authority of the church; particular individual experience; reason based on the total evidence; and the Bible—are interrelated. Within mainstream Christianity no one base should be claimed exclusively over against the others. But is there a possibility that the Bible can again become more central to Christian life?

Basic to understanding the Bible as the foundation of our faith is a return to understanding the Bible as the Word of God—not the words of God, nor simply the words of human beings, but as the Word of God. Word implies address, communication, the possibility of a response and a relationship.

What Is the Bible?

When we ask, "What is the Bible?" the most obvious answer is that the Bible is human words. In fact, the Bible is not one book, but a whole library of books. Sometimes people who are new to the Bible will start at the book of Genesis and try to work their way through to the book of Revelation. Usually when they reach the law codes of Exodus and Leviticus, they get overwhelmed and quit. They feel it is like a dictionary. Reading the Bible is not like reading a novel, starting at the first page and reading through to the end. It's more like approaching a whole bookshelf. One doesn't start at the top left hand corner and work across and down, but rather one looks the books over and then chooses one to read.

The word "bible" is derived from a Greek word, *biblia,* whose original meaning was evidently "books" or a collection of books. *Biblia Sacra,* usually translated "Holy Bible," literally means "sacred books."

There are sixty-six books in the Bible—thirty-nine in "the Old Testament," which was written over a period of at least 800 years, and twenty-seven in "the New Testament," written over a period of about 100 years. In addition, many contemporary translations include the fifteen books of the "Apocrypha," written during the intertestimental period—between the last books of the Old Testament, the Hebrew Scriptures, and the first of the New Testament. These books vary in length from about 300 words to roughly 70,000 words.

At the time most of the Bible was written, edited, or compiled, writing was done on a parchment made from the papyrus plant and rolled onto a roller to form a scroll.

If you take a look at the table of contents of your Bible, you will see that the first five books—Genesis, Exodus, Leviticus, Numbers, and Deuteronomy—are roughly the same length. This is probably because they were originally one continuous narrative. But since it was impractical to have a scroll that would contain all five books, ancient Hebrew scholars and editors divided the scroll into convenient lengths. In the Hebrew Bible the books are simply named by the word with which they begin. Genesis, for instance, a Greek word meaning "beginnings," is called by the Hebrew word with which it begins—*b'resheeth*, meaning "in the beginning."

Look at the last books of the Old Testament, from Isaiah to the end, and you will see that the books of Isaiah, Jeremiah, Ezekiel, and the last twelve books taken together (called in the Hebrew Bible "the Book of the Twelve") are again very roughly the same length, indicating that these too are compilations divided according to the practical length of a scroll. (In the Hebrew Scriptures, the book of Daniel appears in a different place, under "the Writings.")

The Bible contains many kinds of writing—for example, history, 1 and 2 Samuel or 1 and 2 Kings, or in the New Testament, the book of "The Acts of the Apostles"; poetry, the book of Psalms is Hebrew poetry, the "hymn book" of ancient Israel; and correspondence, the letters of Paul and others. It also contains certain types of literature unique to the Bible itself, such as prophecy, wisdom literature, and "apocalyptic literature," for instance, the book of Daniel in the Old Testament and the book of Revelation in the New Testament.

The first thing that is obvious when we begin to study the Bible is that it is composed of human words. The Bible is written in the words of human languages—Hebrew, Greek, and Aramaic. For this reason, we must have the Bible translated into our own language or learn to read Hebrew and Greek so that we can read it in the original languages. Some scholars spend many years becoming proficient in these languages. They write commentaries to give us a deeper understanding of the meaning and implication of the words of the books of the Bible.

The Bible is a book of books, made up of human words. But for the Christian faith, the Bible is not simply human words; it is the Word of God.

Please note that I am not saying it is the "words" of God. Most of us have grown up with a vague belief that the Bible is just that—the words of God. We have been given an impression that it was written as God dictated words to people who acted as scribes and who wrote down, word for word, everything that God said to them. Therefore the whole Bible, letter for letter and word for word, is literally true and must be believed from cover to cover.

Such an understanding of inspiration is ancient, going beyond Christian times, for instance, to some Pharisaical beliefs. In some ways, it is truer of Islamic understanding, how the Ku'ran was inspired, rather than the Christian understanding of how the Bible is inspired. In Islamic understanding, God (Allah) spoke to Muhammad the prophet and instructed him to "recite" exactly what God spoke to him. For Muslims then, the Ku'ran is exactly the words of God (Allah).

An attempt to understand the Bible literally raises, I believe, more problems than it solves. Certainly it raises difficulties for people in this scientific age. How did Jesus turn water into wine? How could Jonah live for three days in the belly of a whale? As we shall see, one may believe the "facts" and miss the message completely.

Anyone who has taken a high school science course is aware that there seems to be a major conflict between the creation story in the Bible and contemporary scientific evolutionary theories of creation. The Bible itself raises all sorts of questions, making difficult any attempt to understand it literally. There are the old catch-questions such as, "Who came first, Adam and Eve or the cave-dwellers?" or "Where did Cain get his wife?" and "Why are the genealogies of Jesus in the Gospels of Matthew and Luke different?"

There are many other such questions that could be asked. Why does David, who in 1 Samuel 16 appears as Saul's armor-bearer and is described as a seasoned warrior, appear in the following chapter as an immature and inexperienced youth who is unknown to Saul and not big and strong enough to wear his armor? In fact, the better you know the Bible and the better you know the languages from which it is translated, the more such questions arise.

Most Christians, through the history of the church, have never tried to understand the whole Bible literally. It has been recognized that there are parts of the Bible that are intended to be historical and other parts of the Bible that are poetic or symbolic. Sometimes the words appear to be simple stories, but stories that make a significant point about God's will and way with us. A long-standing rule in the church was that the Bible should be understood either literally (historically), symbolically (by use of allegory), morally, or mystically (spiritually, especially with reference to the "after life"). The Protestant tradition has preferred a simple, historical interpretation where that is clearly the meaning—in part a reaction against the tendency, through the Middle Ages and back to Origen, one of the church fathers, to find allegorical meanings in every page. Some such allegorical interpretations, though wonderfully imaginative, defied all sense of reason.

I reject the view that the Bible is "the words of God" not because it raises scientific problems or because God must then be said to be self-contradictory, *but because such an understanding of the Bible completely misses the meaning of the phrase "the Word of God."*

The Bible as the Word of God

Lay aside this book for a few minutes and look up some passages in your Bible. First, read Genesis 27. Then turn to the book of Numbers and read chapters 22 through 24. Read also 2 Samuel 23:13–17. Then continue reading here.

Genesis 27: Notice in this account how important it is to Esau to receive his father's blessing. Esau and Jacob were twins, but Esau was born first, and therefore, could claim the right of the first-born (the right of primogeniture whereby the estate passes to the eldest son), to become the head of the clan. Jacob, whose name means "usurper," was born with his hand clutching Esau's heel. This story tells how Jacob, who was later called Israel, and hence the father of the "children of Israel," usurped the father's blessing.

Esau, the rough and ready man of the fields and mountains, wept like a baby because he had been deprived of his father's blessing. Isaac, the father, having spoken the blessing on Jacob, could not repeat it for his first-born son, Esau. It was Jacob he had blessed, " . . . yes, and blessed he shall be" (Genesis 27:33–36).

Numbers 22-24: In this strange story Balak, king of Moab, placed more confidence in the power of the spoken word of the prophet Balaam than he did in his own army. Notice also that Balaam, who was a true prophet, could only speak the words that God gave him. He couldn't pronounce a curse on Israel as Balak wished. He could only bless them. "How can I curse whom God has not cursed?" (Numbers 23:8).

Second Samuel 23:13-17: In this instance, David was in hiding, living in a cave with his "mighty men." It was a time of great discouragement. On one side, the Philistines were out to get him. On the other, Saul, the king, in a jealous madness, was after his life. Remembering the carefree days of his childhood around the well at Bethlehem, and no doubt being physically thirsty in a part of the country where there was little water available, David muttered, "O that someone would give me water to drink from the well of Bethlehem that is by the gate" (2 Samuel 23:15).

Three of the leaders of his force of fighting men then undertook to get what their leader had requested. They found a way through the enemy lines (Bethlehem was in the hands of the Philistines), risking their own lives, just to get the water their leader had desired.

When they returned with the water to David, he simply poured it out upon the ground as a sacrifice to the Lord. "Far be it from me, O Lord, to do this! Is it not the blood of men who went at the risk of their lives?" (2 Samuel 23:17).

What seems to be the outstanding feature that these stories have in common? Isn't it that *words* are understood to have a power in themselves?

The Hebrews held the belief that words did have power in themselves, power to accomplish what they said. Words of blessing did indeed bless, and the expression "God damn you!"—so common in our society—would have been considered a most dangerous and terrible thing to say.

Why? Because, to the Hebrews, a person's "spirit," life, resided in his or her breath. The Hebrew word *nephesh* meant spirit, life, or breath. When people died, their life, their spirit, their breath went out of them.

A word is essentially a puff of breath. It is a going out from the person of her or his spirit. It has power in itself to accomplish what it says, according to the power of the person who spoke it. In the family, the words of Isaac, as patriarch and head of the family or tribe, would have the power to accomplish what he said. In the nation, the king would possess such power. And the prophet, if indeed the prophet was a true prophet and spoke as God commanded, possessed immense power. This is why the father's blessing was so important to Esau. This is why Balak, king of Moab, put so much confidence in the words of Balaam, the prophet, and why the "three mighty men" responded so bravely to David's muttered thoughts.

Now if the power of ordinary mortals, even patriarchs and kings, possessed such power, surely any word of God would be all-powerful. What God said must be so! Notice, in the story of creation that God didn't *do* anything except speak. "Then God said, 'Let there be light'; and there was light" (Genesis 1:3).

Stop a minute and consider this strange Hebrew notion. Perhaps we are apt to think it a bit fantastic, but let's remember that we live in a time that has gone to the other extreme. Ours is an age that emphasizes activity. Our high school and university heroes are the athletes, not the scholars. We admire the person who is always doing something, not the recluse who likes to read a lot.

Have you ever heard it said that the human race has reached its present peak of civilization because it has a thumb and forefingers that meet, thereby making it possible for human beings to use tools? This is sometimes given as the reason for the advantage of human beings over other animals, but surely the tongue is as important as the thumb in whatever progress we have made in this world. "The pen is mightier than the sword," wrote Baron Lytton,[2] and Northrop Frye wrote,

> The Israelites seem to have been a rather unhandy people, not distinguished for architecture or sculpture or even pottery. . . . In general it was the heathen kingdoms that produced the really impressive temples and palaces, while the Israelites produced a book. This doubtless seemed at best only a consolation prize to people who thought of buildings as more substantial than words, but history has long since reversed such a perspective.[3]

And the tongue is the instrument of contemplation, while the thumb is the instrument of action. Remember that the greatest battle going on in the world today is not in the development of armies and armaments. It is the battle of words, of ideas and ideologies. People are finally won by persuasion, not by arms. "The pen is mightier than the sword."

Perhaps the Hebrews were not so far wrong as we might have been inclined to believe. Let us recognize that words do possess a lot of power. It may seem that we are back to talking about "the words of God" rather than "the Word of God." But the Hebrews thought of "the Word of God" as an expression of the will and the power of God, an expression of the Spirit of God. Now think what this means when we turn to the New Testament.

The New Testament Understanding

Turn to the first chapter of the Gospel of John and read the first 14 verses. "In the beginning was the Word, and the Word was with God, and the Word was God!" What does it all mean? Why is "Word" spelled with a capital letter? In the second verse, unless you're using a translation of the Bible that refuses to use the masculine pronoun in reference to God, you'll notice that it says, "*He* was in the beginning with God. All things came into being through *him*, and without *him* not one thing came into being" (emphasis added).

Who is this "*He*"?

By this time you've probably read to the fourteenth verse and figured it all out for yourself. "And the Word became flesh and lived among us, and we have seen his glory, the glory as of a father's only son, full of grace and truth" (John 1:14).

The Bible refers to Jesus as "the Word of God." As words (in Hebrew understanding) are the self-expression of the person who utters them (the going-forth from them, in a puff of breath, of their purpose, their spirit, their heart and mind), so in Jesus Christ we see the going-forth from God of the Spirit of God, the mind and heart of the Creator. Jesus is the complete expression of God's Person, of God's power and love. ". . . and his name is called The Word of God" (Revelation 19:13).

In the first chapter of the Gospel of John, "Word" is translated from the Greek word *logos,* which literally means word. It can also mean the study of a subject, as biology is the study of life and geology the study of the earth. The word theology can mean both "the study of God" and also "the Word of God."

In the Stoic philosophers and in Philo *logos* came to refer to the basic structure on which our existence is formed. We might refer to the laws of life, the reason or pattern or structure of our being. But, as mentioned earlier, "being" in Hebrew tends to have a more dynamic understanding than in Greek. The God of the Bible, the great "I am," is living, not static.

It is the genius of the writer of the fourth Gospel to put together this Hebrew understanding of the Word of God with the Greek meaning of *logos* and to use it in reference to Jesus, God-in-Christ, as "the Word!"

Then why do we call the Bible "the Word of God?" If Jesus is the Word of God, then why do we speak, how *can* we speak, of the Bible as the Word of God? To answer, let's turn to some words of Jesus: "You search the scriptures because you think that in them you have eternal life; and it is they that testify on my behalf" (John 5:39). This verse is sometimes understood to say that we find "eternal life" in the Bible itself. But Jesus is saying to the scribes and Pharisees that they *won't* find eternal life in the Scriptures, because that is not what the Scriptures are for. The Scriptures are to point the way to the One who *can* give eternal life.

Jesus' words on this occasion are directed, according to the testimony of John, against those who, though they may be very religious and hold the Scriptures in reverence, deny the One to whom the Scriptures bear witness, Jesus himself, the personal expression of God's Spirit. "Yet you refuse to come to me to have life," he finished (John 5: 40).

Let's go back to our first question: *What is the Bible?* Is it any more than just a conglomeration of books? Have the books anything in common other than being religious writings out of the Jewish heritage? Is there some unifying theme to the whole Bible?

This is a difficult question and scholars are not altogether united in their answer. However, it is generally true to say that Christian tradition has affirmed that Jesus, whom we call Christ, is the One of whom the whole Bible speaks. This collection of books that we call the Bible from first to last witnesses to Jesus, the One we have said is "the Word of God." The Word was in the beginning with God; it was by the Word of God that the earth and the heavens were made (Psalm 33:6). It was the Word of God that spoke through the law and the prophets. And in the fullness of time, the Word was born of Mary, and "we have seen his glory, the glory as of a father's only son" (John 1:14).

It is true that the Bible consists of human words. It contains history, drama, poetry, and many other kinds of literature. But through the Bible we see the witness to the One who presents to us the full and perfect expression of God's will for humanity, the One known as Jesus of Nazareth, Christ, "the Word of God."

It is for this reason we call the Bible "the Word of God." It *is* the Word because it bears witness to God's Word in Jesus Christ. In pointing beyond itself to him, *it is "the Word."* It is "the power of God for salvation to everyone who has faith. . . . For in it the righteousness of God is revealed through faith for faith; as it is written, 'The one who is righteous will live by faith'" (Romans 1:16–17).

When the words are read, when the story is heard again in faith, it is never merely familiarity with "the facts." It is the power of the living God moving to redeem and to save.

5

LOOKING THROUGH THE
WORDS TO THE WORD

*Seeking an Encounter
with God*

> The Bible is authoritative because it points beyond itself to the
> absolute authority, the living and transcendent Word of God.
>
> Donald Bloesch[1]

he Bible has been described as a telescope —not something
to look *at,* but to look *through.* We must look *through* the
literature of the Bible—the history, the science, the human
speculation—to what the Bible is witnessing to. We must listen
for the Word of God coming to us *through the words.*

Christian faith is rooted in history—the history of the Hebrew
people, the life and ministry of Jesus, and the historical reality of his
resurrection. Yet the Bible is not simply a history or science book.
It was not written in the language of objective, scientific description.
It was written in a more poetic kind of language, in which, as
Northrop Frye describes, "the emphasis falls rather on the feeling
that subject and object are linked by a common power or energy."[2]
This approach, according to Frye, contrasts with our contemporary,
"culturally dominant" use of language as "primarily descriptive of
the natural order,"[3] a dimension fueled largely by the growth of modern science and its emphasis on inductive observation.[4]

Part of our struggle in understanding the Bible is that we try to read it through the lenses of our culturally dominant language of objective, scientific description, although most of the Bible was written in a language of pictures and poetry. Poet Luci Shaw comments:

> Where most prose gives us information or instruction, poetry offers reflection on something *wonder*-full, some event or phenomenon that has caused the poet to express wonder in a way that draws the reader into the wonderful as well.[5]

For instance, when the psalmist states, "I was born guilty, a sinner when my mother conceived me" (Psalm 51:5), he is speaking in poetic, not scientific, language. The implication is that sin seems to be so much a part of me that it goes to the marrow of my bones, back to the moment of my conception. Interpreting this passage as a literal or scientific fact has done much harm to the understanding of human sexuality in both Roman Catholic and Protestant traditions.

In an address in 1975,[6] Frye spoke of "truth of correspondence" where the historical account of an event, "what we might have seen if we had been present at the event," is "judged true if it is a satisfactory verbal replica" of the event. Frye critiqued so-called "literal" statements—accounts of data and detail—as of limited value in contrast to "poetic" statements, which capture the essence of an event. "Words certainly have their descriptive uses, but these are of limited help if we are trying to investigate the kind of world that the Bible seems to lead us to: a world in which truth is a person or a personal God."[7]

Frye went on to say that "there is unmistakably a sense in which the Bible transcends the poetic as well as the historical." The Bible is more than a history book or a work of literature.

> There is a third category: the actual event which is probably nothing like what we should have experienced if we had been "there." The assumption here is that, in some events at least, our ordinary experience does not tell us what is really happening . . . an additional dimension of experience . . . a description of experience as it appears to a higher state of consciousness. . . . In the Gospels, it seems clear that the ordinary experience of those who were "there," including the disciples, took in very little of what the Gospel says was really going on at the time.[8]

Therefore, we must look through the words for the Word. We must listen, not just to the facts, but also to the One who is speaking to us through the facts.[9] Let's take some examples from the Old Testament. First, we will consider the opening chapters of the Bible. These passages have been misunderstood both by those who sought to uphold the Bible and by those who sought to understand it in terms of contemporary scientific theory (the thumpers and the bashers). Then we will look at the book of Jonah, one of the most sublime stories of the Old Testament. If read only in its seemingly literal or historical sense, we miss the message entirely. These are portions of the Bible that are not intended to be historical.

The Story of Adam and Eve, Genesis 2–3: First read these chapters, starting with the last half of the fourth verse of the second chapter of Genesis, which scholars tell us is where "the second creation story" begins.

Do you think this story is true?

If you asked me this question, I would reply emphatically "Yes!" But I might not mean it in the same way that you meant it when you asked the question.

I don't gamble; I bet only on sure things. But I'd be willing to bet that you are asking if the story is true *as history.* Is it true that a man named Adam and a woman named Eve lived in a place called the Garden of Eden somewhere back in history? (According to Archbishop Ussher in the seventeenth century, the world was created in 4004 B.C. [10])

We have trouble believing what is in the Bible not because we find it unbelievable, impossible, but because it seems irrelevant and unimportant. Quite frankly, I don't know whether this story is historically true or not, and I don't think it matters a great deal. According to contemporary historical methods, we cannot know whether this story is true or not. We will claim it is historically true only if we believe it to be a factual historical account of divine origin of the beginnings of humanity. But I would claim that this particular passage was never intended to be understood as history, as we understand history today. Further, what difference does it make, historically, unless you are an historian or an anthropologist? *You can believe the story as history and still miss what it means to understand the Bible as the Word of God.*

When I said that I thought it was true, I meant that I thought it was true to life, to human experience as I have known it. I believe that this story is true personally, of me. I understand it as a statement of religious or spiritual truth rather than historical truth. And I believe that this is not only the way we are to understand it, but also the way we *must* understand it if we are to understand it at all.

If I told you that World War II ended in 1945, you would probably agree without hesitation that I made a true statement, an obvious citation of historical fact. If you live in Egypt or another Islamic country, however, this statement of course would *not* be true. It is true relative *only* to the Christian era. World War II ended in 1945 A.D., or *Anno Domini*, "the year of the Lord." World War II ended for Christians and those who keep track of the years by the Christian calendar in the year of our Lord 1945. By the Muslim calendar, World War II ended 1324 A.H. (after the Hegira, the flight of Muhammad from Mecca to Medina, from which the Muslim calendar is dated).

If I say to you, on another note, that war is a terrible thing, this statement may cause a conversation, even a bit of controversy. Isn't war sometimes necessary, even just? Are there not other things worse than war? Don't wars after all cause some good things to happen? Yet we might finally agree that, even with other factors considered, war is a terrible thing.

Notice that the first of these statements, which we are apt to consider obviously true, is only relatively true, in relation to our own system of counting the years. This is an empirical, or quantitative, statement.

The second statement, "War is a terrible thing," seems initially a more controversial statement, yet insofar as it is true, it is always true. It is a qualitative statement about human values.

The late Robert McAfee Brown provided illuminating insights into the question of "true" statements in his book, *The Bible Speaks To You:*

> Let us make sure we understand that when we are dealing with religious questions and scientific questions, we are dealing with two different ways of describing reality, and that the two should not be confused. Genesis is not a scientific account of the Creation, and should not be so interpreted. It deals with "Why?" and its

answer is "God." Modern science looks at the world and asks "How?" and its answer is that the world slowly evolved—an answer that in no sense undermines belief in God.

Here are four statements:

> Two plus two equals four.
> I love you.
> Babe Ruth hit 619 home runs in his major league career.
> I love you too.

It should be clear that statements one and three are of a different order from statements two and four. One and three are factually verifiable: "you can look them up." Statements two and four cannot be "proved" in the same way; but they can be much "truer" for the meaningful living of life than any number of so-called "factual" statements.[11]

Statements of historical and scientific truth tend to fall into the empirical category of the first statement. Statements of value, morality, and religion tend to fall into the second category, the qualitative statement.[12] It is this latter kind of truth with which the Bible is primarily concerned, and it is in this sense that I said that I thought the story of Adam and Eve to be true.

We need to realize that this is not just a story of a dead ancestor of the distant past, the original great-grandfather of us all, whose wife led him to sin against God and as a consequence we all must pay the penalty. (That's a neat way of blaming someone else for what we know to be our own fault.) The Hebrew word "Adam" simply means humanity. It is related to the Hebrew word *adhamah*, meaning earth. The intimation is that "Adam," humankind, is created of the earth, dust—and yet is also created "in the image of God."

Now do you see what the story is saying? *"Adam" is you and me.* This story is about each one of us. It is the story of how we destroy our innocence, how we break our relationship with God. It is the story of how we, in seeking to become like gods, only end up trying to deny that we are human. (Read Isaiah 5:1–2 for a good synopsis of the story of Adam and Eve.)

Now the story becomes as up-to-date as today's newspaper. Now it takes on a keen relevance, perhaps too keen a relevance for many of us. Now we can understand why this story might not only be said to be true, but it also takes on a power that causes us to think of it as the Word of God.

The Story of Creation, Genesis 1: Recently, in a church service, we were reading Psalm 104. When we got to verse 5, "You set the earth on its foundations," I was surprised to find that I almost said "axis" instead of foundations. Of course, because today our understanding is that the earth turns on its axis rather than standing on a foundation. The Old Testament continually speaks of God "laying the foundation of the earth" (note Job 38:4; Isaiah 48:13). But today our understanding of the universe has changed.

Do you believe that the earth is round instead of flat? Do you believe then that the earth travels in a great orbit around the sun rather than the earth being the center of the universe, and that the stars are not lights hanging in the sky, but other great suns far off in space? Then you do not believe the Bible—at least you don't accept the scientific understanding of the universe, the worldview, given us in the Bible.

The picture we have in this opening chapter of the Bible (the cosmology, or better the cosmogony, of Genesis) is of a more or less flat earth. Over the earth God placed "a dome," a very solid sky—the Hebrew word means "to beat out with a hammer," like sheet metal. In the dome, God attached the sun and the moon and the stars and moved them about according to the times and seasons. God "brings out their host and numbers them, calling them all by name" (Isaiah 40:26; note Psalm 19:4–6).

Over the dome and under the earth are still the salt seawaters of primeval chaos (Genesis 1:6–7). In the story of the great flood, the waters came from both under the earth and from over the dome (Genesis 7:11). Creation was a little pocket of order in an eternal chaos of swirling seawater. "The galaxies and this very planet were brought into existence out of watery chaos by God's word. Then God's word brought the chaos back in a flood that destroyed the world" (2 Peter 3:5–6 THE MESSAGE).

The three-storied universe of the Bible is not heaven, earth, and the fires of hell beneath, but "the heavens above, the earth beneath, and the waters under the earth" (Deuteronomy 5:8; Exodus 20:4).

So many people become confused when they study contemporary scientific theories of how the created order came to be. Evolutionary theories and the Big Bang theory seem to contradict the biblical account. Creationists assert a cosmogony in defiance of current scientific theories. *Actually, the whole debate between evolutionism and creationism is irrelevant to what the Bible is saying about the creation of the universe.* If we read the Bible simply as a science book, it is true that theories of an evolutionary creation do conflict with the biblical account of creation. It's not that the Bible is bad science, it is simply a more primitive worldview, which we do not have today. As a result of this misunderstanding, many people have come to believe that the Bible is irrelevant in their search for truth.

My point is that the biblical account of creation, as a worldview, *is* different from our present understanding. Of course, realize also that our scientific understanding of the universe and how things came to be as they are may be as different 2,000 years hence as our understanding today is different from that of our ancestors.

But just as the story of Adam and Eve uses a primitive story of the first man and woman to bring us a deep and eternal truth about ourselves, so this opening chapter of the first book of the Bible uses a primitive scientific understanding of the world to say certain things that are primarily religious statements.

Read Genesis 1 again and ask yourself what it tells you about God, about the world God created, and about God's purpose in creating humankind. Ask not the scientific question "How?" but the religious question "Why?" It's not an easy question, and you shouldn't expect an immediate answer—but at least you will now be asking the right question. When you ask "Why?" you may then be brought back to the who, the God who created.

There are other ancient stories of creation—Akkadian, Babylonian, and others—but the story of Genesis is unique; God's Word is sovereign. God speaks, and it is so. It is an orderly creation, and God looks on all that has been created, and "it is very good." (Generally, most religions understand the created order as evil rather than good.) The climax of the creative process is the creation of the human being to whom God gives responsibility for the care and keeping of creation.

Read as well Psalm 33:6–9, Hebrews 11:3, and 2 Peter 3:5–7. It is the same Word that is revealed in fullness in Jesus Christ who created the world in the beginning.

Now we may begin to understand ourselves not as a speck of unimportant matter in an immense universe, but as children of a loving Father.

In both the story of creation (Genesis 1) and the story of Adam and Eve (Genesis 2–3), it's not what is said about history or science that is important. It's what is said about God, or better, what God is saying to us. And even though this is the very beginning of the Bible, it may help us to understand the way we must approach the whole Bible.

The tragedy of Jonah, the man who wouldn't forgive: Read Jonah 1; 2:1, 10; 3:1–6, 10; 4:1, 4–11. It will also help to read Matthew 5:43–46; 6:14–15.

Jonah was the man who was swallowed by the "whale," you may remember. There is no more tragic or comic figure in the Bible. In fact, Jonah is, other than our Lord himself, the most misunderstood individual in the whole Bible. The tragedy is not that he was swallowed by a whale—that's only incidental to the story—but that he wouldn't forgive.

No book in the Bible is more misunderstood and unappreciated than this short book of four chapters, tucked away among the minor prophets of the Old Testament. "This is the tragedy of the book of Jonah," writes George Adam Smith in his commentary, "that a book which is the means of one of the most sublime revelations of truth in the Old Testament should be known to most only for its connection with a whale."[13]

Some parts of the Bible are presented as historical; some are not. The book of Jonah is not historical. How long, O Lord, how long will we go on tinkering as technicians as though the Word of God were a jigsaw puzzle, as though by dissecting it with knives and scalpels and prosaic minds we might come to some infallible understanding of what it is saying? How long before we will realize the lightness of the touch of God's grace, the very humor of the manner in which God so often provides the revelation of grace and truth?

This is not a matter simply of strength of belief. It is no more fantastic that a man should be thrown into the sea, swallowed by a great fish, and after three days in the belly of the fish come out unharmed, than that a man should be crucified, have a spear thrust in his side, spend three days in a tomb walled in by a great stone, and then emerge alive with the stone rolled away. As far as belief is concerned, one is about as difficult to believe as the other.

But the whole point of the resurrection of Jesus Christ is that it is an event that happened in history—perhaps at the very boundaries of history, but an event that impinged itself on our empirical experience. As far as the story of Jonah is concerned, it was never intended as an historical account of an incident in Israel's life. It is rather a satirical gem, a prophetic sermon more incisively deadly than all of the great stones hurled by the prophet Amos. Understood in this way, it is the Word of God, the message of God's grace, truth, and mercy.

For a very long time Assyria was the overlord of the Israelite people, and one of the harshest and cruelest of them all. The Jews have always been a freedom-loving people, a people who rebelled against servitude and vassalism. In fact, they caused so much trouble that they were deported and taken into exile. Jerusalem itself was destroyed—Mount Zion and the temple—that which the people earnestly believed that God would never allow to be destroyed.

I suggested that the book of Jonah is not historical. However, there is a reference to Jonah the son of Amittai in 2 Kings 14. Jonah was evidently a man who lived during the reign of Jeroboam II. Scholars suggest, and I believe rightly, that this book of Jonah was *not* written during the reign of Jeroboam II. It was written at a later date, *after* the exile, after the people came back and began to form a new nation and to reestablish themselves in their native land. Under the leadership of Ezra and Nehemiah, they sought to build a "righteous kingdom" according to strict adherence to the ancient law.

If you read the biblical accounts of this period, you will realize just how earnest and sincere the Israelites were. Every jot and tittle of the law must be kept and followed, that this time no mistake would be made. There should be no possibility that God would once again punish them. This was carried even to inhuman extremes.

One of the qualities that developed in Israel during this period was a hatred of their enemies, in fact of all non-Israelites. This

hatred was never greater than when directed at the Assyrians—
and the capital of Assyria was Nineveh.

To understand, go to those ancient ruins in the Persian desert
and study the miles of carving and painting on the ruins of the
walls of ancient cities showing masses of troops marching on some
long-gone city or other fortification—enormous engines of destruc-
tion pushed up to the walls under a covering rain of arrows, streets
and palaces strewn with corpses, men impaled by spears and children dashed against the stones. It would have been difficult not to
hate the Assyrians.

Assyria was known as "the besieger," and Nineveh was known
as "the bloody city." Thus, we can understand why the people of
Israel of that time had become so concerned to preserve their purity.
It was to this situation that the book of Jonah was written—set
back in imagination to the time of Jeroboam II to give it acceptance. The Hebrew name "Jonah" means "dove," and the dove
was a symbol of the Israelite people. "Jonah" is presented as the
typical Hebrew of the time, the personification of the Israelite people. Understood in this way, the book of Jonah becomes not just
an incident back in Hebrew history, but the very Word of God,
speaking with power and relevance even to us today.

God came to Jonah and said, in effect, "I'm going to destroy
Nineveh. Her evil has come before me, her violence and her corruption. I'm fed up with it!" Now Jonah, as a typical Israelite, would
be delighted to hear that God was going to destroy Nineveh. But
then God said to Jonah, "And I want you to go there and preach,
and to tell them that I am going to destroy them." Jonah thought
to himself, "If I go and tell them what God is going to do to them,
perhaps they will repent. And I know what God is like—a God of
compassion and mercy. If the Ninevites repent, then probably God
won't destroy them after all." (This, of course, was the last thing
in the world that any Israelite would want to happen.)

So Jonah went down to the seaport of Joppa, chancing the dan-
gers of crossing the Philistine territory along the way. There he
bought a ticket on a ship going to the other end of the Mediter-
ranean Sea, to Tarshish (Spain), as far away as he could get from
Nineveh. Keep in mind that the Israelites were a land-loving people who avoided sea travel with a passion. Jonah's action would
have excited the interest and the sympathy of a people who would

have liked to think that they might take the same kind of des-
perate action. "Go to Nineveh to preach repentance? Why, yes,
I'd rather take a ship for Tarshish myself, any day."

But the Lord sent a great wind and the whole ship was in dan-
ger. Jonah knew that the Lord had sent the wind, because he was
running away from the Lord. So when the storm came up, Jonah
went down into the hold of the ship and fell asleep.

The captain of the ship went down into the ship and woke Jonah.
"You pray too, brother, for maybe your prayers will help us out.
Maybe your God is of some influence in whatever is going on here."
Of course Jonah knew what was going on—he knew that he was
the cause of the storm. So when the sailors cast lots to see who was
to blame, Jonah was not surprised when the lot fell to him.

In fact, Jonah encouraged the sailors to cast him into the sea
so that they and the ship might be saved. The intimation is that
Jonah would rather die than see the lives of the sailors sacrificed.
Once again, you see how the story would excite the sympathy of
the Israelite people. Jonah would rather die than go to Nineveh
and be the means of saving the hated city.

Finally, after some hesitation, the sailors did throw Jonah to
the waves, but Jonah didn't die. He only discovered what he
should already have known—it's not so easy to escape the Lord
God and his divine will.

> Where shall I go from your spirit?
> Or where can I flee from your presence?
> If I ascend to heaven, you are there;
> if I make my bed in sheol, you are there.
> If I take the wings of the morning and settle at the farthest limits
>   of the sea, even there Your hand shall lead me,
> and your right hand shall hold me fast.
>
> Psalm 139:7–10

God sent a "great fish." The sea, to the ancient Hebrews, was
the symbol of primeval chaos. It was filled with all sorts of mon-
sters. The point is not that Jonah spent three days in the belly of
the fish and lived to tell about it, but that the fish was God's means
of bringing Jonah back, depositing him back on the shores he had
so recently left, where the Word of the Lord first came to him. He

could not so easily escape the call God had placed upon him. And, in one sense, the story begins all over again.

The Word of the Lord came to Jonah a second time. And Jonah, not too anxious to suffer again what he had just been through and realizing that the Lord certainly was not fooling, made his steps, however reluctantly, to Nineveh. There he began to parade through the streets of Nineveh and the vast spreading suburbs of the city, walking day by day, calling out that Nineveh in forty days would be destroyed. (The number "forty" is a Hebrew idiom meaning a fairly long period of time.)

To Jonah's horror, the thing he most dreaded happened. The Ninevites did repent. From the king down to the children and the cattle, they turned from their accustomed wickedness and violence, put on sackcloth, fasted, and earnestly prayed to God to forgive them.

There was only one hope left for Jonah. Perhaps the Lord would destroy Nineveh in spite of the repentance of the people. Surely after all the cruelty and bloodshed the people of Nineveh had caused the Lord would not let them off that easily.

So Jonah made himself a crude shelter outside the city on a little hill. He sat there, day by day, waiting to see if the fire of God would descend on Nineveh. Getting angrier with each passing day as he sat in the hot and blazing sun, Jonah gradually realized that God was not going to destroy Nineveh after all. And *he* had been the means of saving "the bloody city." Instead of Nineveh being burned up, Jonah was.

> Lord, didn't I say before I left home that this is just what you would do? That's why I did my best to run away to Spain! I knew that you are a loving and merciful God, always patient, always kind, and always ready to change your mind and not punish. Now then, Lord, let me die. I am better off dead than alive.
>
> Jonah 4:2–3 TEV

Then followed the final blow. The Lord now sent a vine, which grew up over Jonah and provided him with welcome shade from the scorching sun. The vine, which grew miraculously in one day, was eaten the next day by a worm that the Lord sent. To top it off, the Lord also sent a scorching wind from out of the east.

After the sun had risen, God sent a hot east wind, and Jonah was about to faint from the heat of the sun beating down on his head. So he wished he were dead. . . . And God said, "What right have you to be angry about the plant?" Jonah replied, "I have every right to be angry—angry enough to die!"

> The Lord said to him, "This plant grew up in one night and disappeared the next; you didn't do anything for it, and you didn't make it grow—yet you feel sorry for it! How much more, then, should I have pity on Nineveh, that great city. After all, it has more than 120,000 innocent children in it, as well as many animals!"
>
> Jonah 4:8–11 TEV

And so the story ends. It's like a mirror being held up in front of the Israelites of the time. It's a sermon on the text, "Love your enemies." Remember Jesus' words: "If you forgive others their trespasses, your heavenly Father will also forgive you; but if you do not forgive others, neither will your Father forgive your trespasses" (Matthew 6:14–15).

Jonah would not forgive. He wanted God's favor for Israel, but not for Nineveh. He wanted God's grace for himself, but not for others. But Israel was chosen by God to be "a light to the nations" (Isaiah 42:6). She, who had suffered so much at the hand of foreigners, was to be the means of their salvation. It was God's way.

We, who belong to Christ, must never forget that our faith is not so much a matter of getting our own soul saved, but of being the means of God's redemptive and healing love to the world God "so loves." *Hear the Word of the Lord!*

The Bible and History

Christianity is rooted in history. Unless there is actuality behind the events recorded in the Bible, from the exodus to the resurrection, our "faith is futile" (1 Corinthians 15:17). However history, as we find it in the Bible, is not the objective study of the facts as a modern historian might seek to do, dependent upon correspondence with external criteria.

These examples from the Old Testament should never have been understood as history. But much of the Old Testament and much of the New Testament are presented as historical accounts of what happened when. Even here, the point is not in believing the history exactly as it is recorded but in hearing the Word in the history, through the words. (When the history of his story touches the mystery of my story, the "Aha" of faith may occur.)

Take for instance the historical accounts of the life of David, "the most extensively narrated single story" in the Old Testament.[14] Why is this? Why is David so important? Why is Jesus so often named in the New Testament as "son of David?" Certainly the biblical accounts don't try to whitewash their heroes. David's life was reprehensible in many ways. In *Leap Over A Wall*, an excellent study of the life of David, Eugene Peterson writes,

> The David story, like most other Bible stories, presents us not with a polished ideal to which we aspire but with a rough-edged actuality in which we see humanity being formed—the *God* presence in the *earth/human* conditions. . . . David deals with God. As an instance of humanity in himself, he isn't much. He has little wisdom to pass on to us on how to live successfully. He was an unfortunate parent and an unfaithful husband. From a purely historical point of view he was a barbaric chieftain with a talent for poetry. But David's importance isn't in his morality or his military prowess but in his experience of and witness to God. Every event in his life was a confrontation with God.[15]

In the New Testament, the fourth Gospel, John, is quite different from Matthew, Mark, and Luke (often called "the synoptic Gospels" because they are so similar). Events recorded in John are quite different. The chronology of Jesus' ministry is very different (some ten months instead of three years). This Gospel was probably written some thirty or forty years after the other Gospels. One might say that the others were photos and the Gospel of John a portrait, an interpretation. Yet scholars regard this Gospel as more historically accurate in some ways than the others, and Christian tradition generally has regarded it as the deepest, truest understanding of Jesus' ministry of all the Gospels.

Bible scholar William Barclay identified two ways of reading the Gospel of John. One is superficially, as a straightforward account of historical incidents, for the "facts." The other way is to seek to perceive an inner meaning by thinking about and meditating on the incidents:

> Always in the Fourth Gospel there are two things. There is a simple surface story that anyone can understand and retell; but there is also a wealth of deeper meaning for the one who has the eagerness to search and the eye to see and the mind to understand.[16]

Take, for instance, John 2:1–11, the wedding in Cana of Galilee, when Jesus turned water into wine. The essential thing in this incident is not that Jesus turned water into wine once upon a wedding (again, we can believe the facts but miss the meaning), but that wherever the Spirit of Jesus comes into a human life there is a new quality of life. The Spirit of Jesus may turn a life that is ordinary, flat, and dull into something exciting, satisfying and fulfilling, what John himself called "eternal life" (by which he meant not just life after death, but the quality of life which can begin now in our present life). It's like turning water into wine. Remember Jesus' words, "I came that they may have life, and have it abundantly" (John 10:10).

Finally, consider the resurrection of Jesus. What difference does it make? That it happened is very difficult to deny. Someone has said that if there were as much evidence that Julius Caesar visited America we wouldn't doubt it.

At one point in my faith development and theological training I found it very difficult to accept the resurrection as historical fact. I tended to believe that it was the result of some kind of mass hysteria. Yet the more I studied the Scriptures, the more I found myself overpowered by the evidence there. The more I questioned the scriptural witness, the more difficulty I found denying its validity.

I'm not sure we will ever understand exactly what happened or how it happened. It was quite evidently a very visible presence, a "body" of some sort with some kind of objective reality. But it was also and quite obviously not simply a physical body, at least in the sense we commonly use the word "physical."

I find myself frustrated by the arguments whether Jesus' resurrection was physical or spiritual. Some people assert that it was only spiritual. Then others reply that we must believe in "a literal physical resurrection." I suggest to you that such argumentation is vain and the issue is null and void. We simply cannot comprehend the reality of what happened by the words "spiritual" and "physical" as we tend to use them and understand them today.

Whatever this "body" was, it seems obvious that it was not simply a physical resurrection. It was not the resuscitation of a corpse, a dead body come back to life. It was something more. If it had been simply a physical resuscitation and no more, it seems reasonable to suppose that there would have been simply the resumption of their former relationship, a return to what had been before. But it was obviously something very different.

On the other hand, it was not merely spiritual. It wasn't a vague awareness of a spiritual presence that dawned gradually upon them. It hit them quite unexpectedly, like a bolt out of the blue! It was Jesus who appeared to them. It was *really* him!

"Touch me and see!" he said to them in Luke's account. It's as though Luke wants to drive home to us the fact that it was not merely spiritual. Jesus invited them to touch him. He wanted them to know for sure that he was not just a spirit. "A ghost does not have flesh and bones as you see that I have" (Luke 24:39). In John's Gospel (John 20:19–29), Jesus invited Thomas to thrust his finger into the nail prints in his hands and to thrust his hands into the hole in Jesus' side. It's evident that these evangelists, in spite of all the faults and discrepancies of the various narratives, were trying very hard to say that it was not merely a spiritual apparition.

And it changed the whole course of their living, thinking, and expectations. It turned their lives upside down and inside out. Why?

Obviously they themselves had great difficulty in understanding. For them, it meant that the Messiah had come—but a strange Messiah indeed. It meant that life was triumphant over death. But not every life, only the life of this man. Only gradually did they come to realize that by sharing in that same quality of life they knew in Jesus, they too could have "eternal life." But what is that quality of life, and how did they share in it?

It was by the same means we may share in it today—through a relationship with God through the grace of Jesus, by faith, which is based primarily on the Word of God, witnessed by prophets and apostles, in the book we call the Bible. How we enter into and live out this faith, and what the results may be, form the substance of the rest of the book you are now reading.

6

INVITATION TO
A RELATIONSHIP

Discovering the
Unconditional Grace of God

Just as I am Thou wilt receive,
Wilt welcome, pardon, cleanse, relieve;
Because Thy promise I believe,
O Lamb of God, I come.

Charlotte Elliot[1]

The Word of God through the Bible is the basis of our faith and our relationship with God. It is also the invitation to this relationship. Through the Word, God invites us to a relationship with him and with one another.

To be created in the image of God is to be created to responsible relationship with God, and "our hearts are restless till they find their rest in Thee." Yet we seem to find faith so difficult. In my own search for God, over a couple of years I prayed, fasted, read, and went from one church to another. "Surrender," people said. "Let go and let God." But the more *I* tried to surrender, to let go, the more *I* got in the way. My "self" could not give itself completely. Finally I gave up and said, "Lord, you have to take me as I am!"

And of course, the amazing thing is that God did just that.

An Amazingly Simple Gospel

The message of the Bible is simple. Through the years, it has spoken to all people with the good news: "Jesus loves me, this I know, for the Bible tells me so." It's so straightforward, yet many people make it complicated by setting conditions on God's grace.

When I was searching for faith and visiting churches of various denominations, I stopped one Sunday evening at a little Salvation Army hall in the town of Glace Bay, on Cape Breton Island. During a time for "testimonies" (personal witnesses by people to their faith), a little old lady stood and sang a gospel song in a thin, wavering voice, "Life is like a mountain railroad." She was obviously someone to whom life had not been kind. Her singing was so pitiful that a cynic might have laughed—but I have never forgotten it. Here was an uneducated woman whose life had been captured by the gospel message. She stood and sang in triumph.

How would you put the gospel, this Word of God, in your own words? Have you ever tried developing your own "credo," to pray into, think through, and write out what you mean by the gospel? Not in the familiar words of ancient creeds, nor in the slogans of contemporary piety, but what you really believe about life, God, and about Jesus whom we call Lord and Savior?

Having set you up, I'll give you my own answer. I will, as clearly and simply as I can, tell you my understanding of the gospel. It may not agree exactly with your understanding, but that's okay; no two of us have exactly the same experience or see things exactly the same way. My understanding of the gospel may seem quite different, and it may even shock or disturb you. All I ask is that you give my words a hearing.

The word *gospel* means "good news." What we often hear from pulpits, from radio preachers and TV evangelists, doesn't sound like good news. It speaks of conditions on the grace of God in Jesus Christ, conditions that seem more like bad news than good news and seem more likely to inspire fear in our hearts rather than faith. And fear, not doubt, is the antithesis of faith. (Doubt, in the biblical sense, is more a kind of existential anxiety than intellectual questioning.)

The "gospel" is the good news of God's grace in Jesus Christ the Lord. It is the good news that "in Christ God was reconciling the world" (2 Corinthians 5:19). To reduce it to its simplest expression, the gospel is that "God is gracious"—God is good and just. This may seem a simple statement, but it has great implications. If God is good and God is just, then God will do what is good and right for each one of us. And we can ask for nothing more. It means that I can trust myself and those I love to God's gracious care and keeping—in sickness and health, in life and death.

> What can separate us from the love of Christ? Trouble or pain? Persecution? Lack of clothing or food? Danger to life or threat of war? . . . No! In all these, we are more than conquerors through the One who loves us. For I am absolutely convinced that there is nothing—neither death nor life, neither spiritual power nor physical violence, in the world as it is or the world as it shall be, nothing in all the universe, in the heights of the sky or the depths of the earth, which can separate us from the love of God which is in Jesus Christ our Lord.
>
> Romans 8:35–39, my own translation

The primary biblical meaning of faith is not so much what we believe but in whom we believe. Because God is good and God is just, we can trust God. We can trust ourselves into his care. This is "salvation"—to live in confidence that the ultimate nature of nature is benevolent, in spite of the sometimes seemingly angry face of the natural world. And this is peace, the peace that passes all understanding. "Thou wilt keep him in perfect peace, whose mind is stayed on thee: because he trusteth in thee" (Isaiah 26:3 KJV).

This does not mean that salvation is an automatic process by which we are all saved no matter what we believe or what we do. The judgment of God is very real, but it is merciful, and its purpose is redemptive, intended not to punish or destroy but to save.

> I see the wrong that round me lies,
> I feel the guilt within;
> I hear, with groan and travail-cries,
> The world confess its sin.
> Yet in the maddening maze of things,
> And tossed by storm and flood,
> To one fixed trust my spirit clings:
> I know that God is good.[2]

If People Dispensed God's Grace

A central theme of human religion is getting God to do what we want, getting him to serve us. This is true whether it is ancient gods for whom people performed sometimes hideous sacrifices in their fear and need, or the God to whom even we turn for help or happiness. The prayer is often trivial—for help in an exam for which we haven't studied; for our team to win a ball game; or for money to buy a dress or ball glove. "O God, live among us, serve us and give us our desires. Keep Willy out of trouble, introduce Muriel to a handsome naval officer, and grant that I don't get caught and live forever. Amen."[3] We also pray for deeper things— courage to do the right thing, healing for loved ones in sickness— but which, while evidently good, are still a matter of getting what we want from God.

Of course, we who are so small and powerless in the face of the powers of the universe are going to want God's help and God's protection. But when our religion consists solely of attempts to get what we want out of God, there is something sadly lacking in our faith. Yet, for many people isn't faith precisely our trust that God will give us what we ask for, whether healing from disease, or getting our children well married and settled, or getting our own souls saved (which, however religious, can itself be an expression of loveless selfishness)? And beyond getting saved, we have claimed means of grace, as though the grace of God might be a commodity parceled out in response to our devotion. In this process, we act as though the grace of God is conditional upon some action or procedure on our part.

Sometimes people have said that getting God's grace is a matter of belonging to the right church, possessing the correct ecclesiastical connections, and receiving the sacraments and ministries of the church through the proper channels of apostolic succession and valid ordination.

Some claim that it's getting saved according to the right and valid psychological or religious experience. It's coming forward at the altar call and having the right kind of feeling so you can boast that you're a "born-again believer." Or it's a matter of being baptized with the Holy Spirit and speaking in tongues.

Or it's a matter of right doctrine, correct belief—the Apostles' Creed, or the Westminster Confession, or the Augsburg Confession, or the Thirty-nine Articles of the Church of England, or believing the Bible from cover to cover. In ancient times, the church formed "the Athanasian Creed" which, after a very complex statement of Christian doctrine, ended with the words, "This is the true and Catholic faith, which unless a man believe it, he has no hope of salvation." It's a good creed, but if you don't understand it, can you really believe it?

For many in the mainline Protestant churches, it seems to be a matter of minimum morality and religious respectability. As long as you don't get caught stealing from the company, or get drunk on Saturday night and beat up your wife, and as long as you go to church on Sunday morning when it's convenient, then you are the kind of good, respectable citizen God will be pleased to take in when the time comes.

Notice that the inevitable result of such understandings of grace is both divisive and self-centered. It is divisive because *I* must be right. Those who don't believe as I believe, who don't go to my church, who have not had the same kind of religious experience, who don't manifest the same kind of attitudes and opinions must all be *wrong*. If they are right, then I am wrong, and my very salvation is at stake. I must prove that I am right, even if it means forming a new fellowship—the one, true church.

And it is self-centered in that it is concerned with saving *my* soul. Notice in the more pietistic traditions how often the first-person pronoun appears. "Blessed assurance, Jesus is *mine*."

But how can heaven be heaven if we have no hope for those we have loved on earth? Remember in the book of Genesis, Judah's cry when Joseph required that he leave Benjamin as forfeit: "How can I go back to my father if the boy is not with me?" (Genesis 44:34). How can anyone in Christian love want to go to heaven if those we love are going to hell? Many times I have talked to a woman who has just lost her husband, often after a happy marriage of many years. "He was a good man," she might say—but behind her eyes I could see the question, the fear. Her husband, though a good man and well respected in the community, had not gone to church. What would happen to her husband now? Would she ever see and know him again? Was it possible that he had gone to hell?

The grace of Jesus Christ is not merely a means of getting our own souls saved, of getting into heaven. It stands in opposition to all human schemes of assurance. Remember Jesus' words, "For those who want to save their life [or soul] will lose it" (Matthew 16:25). And in what we have called "the Parable of the Last Judgment" (Matthew 25:31–46), it is those who are so sure that they are saved who are cast into utter darkness.

Our assurance is not in any human means, but simply and solely in God's Word, the grace of Jesus Christ. It is the goodness and justice of God that we see in the cross of Christ. It's as though we're being told, "Stop trying to save yourself! God is gracious! Trust in that. You need do nothing more." In Jesus Christ, God has given his Word.

This is the basis of the relationship, the Word of God. There is nothing we must do, nothing we can do, except to enter into the relationship with God and begin to walk each day with a sense of God's presence and in the knowledge of his love. Remember again the saying of Augustine in his *Confessions,* "Thou hast made us for Thyself, and our hearts are restless till they find their rest in Thee." We are created in the image of God, for relationship with God, and we are not at peace until we make our peace with God.

It's not even necessary that we acknowledge our sin. The traditional evangelistic requirement to acknowledge that I am a sinner can result in what the Protestant Reformers called "legal repentance," a belief that we cannot be acceptable to God until we have realized our sin, which is commonly understood as wrong moral actions. Instead the Reformers affirmed "evangelical repentance," realizing that when a person comes to know the face of God, the grace of God-in-Christ in the reality of the cross, he or she will then realize what sin is and repentance will be from the heart.

Walk each day with a sense of God's presence, and in the confidence of God's love. It's really so simple—don't make it complicated. Enter in. It is God in the grace of our Lord Jesus Christ who invites us.

Faith and Feelings

One thing I especially crave—that anyone who reads these words may know God's presence in grace and truth even when God seems gone. We are too apt to associate our faith with our

feelings, as if God or the Holy Spirit is a certain feeling. Many of
us, when we first turn to God and find peace with God, experience a wonderful sense of exhilaration and aliveness. But faith is
not a feeling, and it is faith we live by, not feelings. A spiritual
high does not last, and if that is the basis of our faith, we soon
flounder.

We have noted how in the nineteenth century, when confidence
in the Bible, the church, and the revelation of God in creation were
under attack, it seemed the only sure refuge for faith was in one's
subjective experience. The emphasis was strongly on religious experience—on feelings, rebirth and the assurance of salvation. What
I know in my heart no one can deny. Revivals were the order of
the day, so that the excitement and the emotion of the early days
of one's religious experience could be rediscovered. There are still
many churches where the purpose of Sunday worship seems to be
to stir up the emotions in order to recreate the experience of the
baptism of the Spirit of God. The result is an overemphasis on
emotion, and this has had some regrettable results.

I remember one woman on my mission field in the bush country of Saskatchewan who told me of the agonies she went through
for a year before she *felt* saved. A whole year of praying and weep-
ing, while her children went without proper meals and had only
uncertain care. I have known people who died in torment because
they were not able to *feel* forgiven.

There are many people who come to a place in their lives where
in a deep spiritual experience they make their peace with God and
perhaps have a climactic born-again experience. They experience
a spiritual exhilaration that may last weeks or even months. But
then comes a time when the feeling leaves and they feel aban-
doned. Maybe they plod through it, but sometimes they quit, con-
cluding that it was all an illusion because the feeling has gone.

We aren't brought into a right relationship with God by the
way we feel, but "by grace through faith" (Ephesians 2:8). The
presence of God's Spirit in our hearts is not dependent on whether
we're having a good day or whether we feel happy. If God's presence in our lives were dependent on feelings, it would mean that
those Monday morning blues are a sign that our faith is no good
and the Spirit of God is no longer with us. It would mean that we
could pray only when we feel God near. It's when we don't feel

that God is near that we need to pray! It would mean going to church only when we feel God is near.

In my own search for God, I never did have the kind of born again experience that I expected and sought. Now I am convinced that that particular kind of experience was not for me, that it was God's intention for me to realize that the reality of faith is not dependent on any certain kind of religious or emotional experience or feeling. The result has been that I have been able to help others realize that their faith is real, even if they haven't had the kind of religious experience some talk about.

Faith is based on something outside and apart from ourselves, on what happened that first Christmas, that first Good Friday, and that first Easter. It is not dependent upon our subjective feelings.

We are so often worried about our faith. "I don't have much faith!" "My faith is so weak!" But when we know the grace of God, we realize that we don't have to worry about whether we have enough faith, or whether we have the right faith. It is accepting the fact that God in Jesus Christ has called and chosen us. Remember Jesus' words to his disciples, "You did not choose me but I chose you" (John 15:16). Our choice of God is important, for it takes two to enter into a relationship. But "while we still were sinners Christ died for us" (Romans 5:8). God accepts us just as we are, not on condition that we get rid of all our bad habits. "Just as I am, without one plea, but that Thy blood was shed for me!" This hymn, by Charlotte Elliott, sung during the altar call at many evangelistic services, is still an excellent statement of the reality of God's call to each of us. It is said of the author that "she gathered up in her soul the great certainties, not of her emotions but of her salvation."[4]

There was a time in my ministry when, after some twenty-five years of intensive pressure in large, multi-staff congregations and a few years in university ministry during the radical 1960s, I felt worn out physically and dry spiritually. So I took a year off.

That summer our family lived on Saturna Island, the most southeasterly of the Gulf Islands of British Columbia, across the border from the San Juan Islands of Washington State. We stayed in a house overlooking the water. Each morning I would get up early, before the others, and sit on the patio overlooking the water sparkling in the morning sun.

I had no sense of God's presence. I couldn't even pray. I was spiritually dry and empty.

Down by the shore stood two arbutus trees, quite common to the Gulf Islands. Arbutus trees have a strange, reddish bark and glossy leaves that catch the light and shine in the sun. Each morning I would sit and look at those trees, shining in the morning sun. They were for me a kind of theophany, a sign or manifestation of God's presence when I couldn't feel anything spiritually. Those trees got me through those first weeks.

But it is significant that the God whose presence I saw in those trees was not some animistic spirit of a god of nature, but the God I knew in Jesus Christ, through the Word of God which had come to me through the Bible. Since the Word of God through the Bible was such an important part of my past, it helped to get me through that present desert of the soul. I think, in the long run, habits are more important than feelings.

As we begin to think about how we respond to God through Scripture, prayer, and worship, it's important to remember that our faith is based not upon our feelings but upon the foundation of the Bible as the Word of God. Whatever our outward circumstances, whatever our psychological state, happy or sad, sickness or health, life or death, we may know that "nothing in all creation, will be able to separate us from the love of God in Christ Jesus our Lord" (Romans 8:39).

Habits of Faith

Brenda and I have reached that stage of our lives when we are reading once again, this time to our grandchildren, those children's stories that form part of the history of our culture—"Goldilocks and the Three Bears," "The Three Little Pigs," and the others. In more mature years, I began to realize that these stories often have a deeper meaning that is sometimes subtle or ambiguous.

Take "The Three Little Pigs." Each one of us in our living builds a house in which we live. Some of us build with straw, and some with sticks, but some build a house with bricks and mortar that can stand the most furious gales that the wolves of life can blow upon it. Jesus told the parable of two men, one wise and one foolish. The wise man built his house upon the rock, and in the storms of life the house stood firm. The foolish man built his house upon the sand, and the winds blew and the rains came down and washed that house away (Matthew 7:24–27).

We tend to look for easy solutions and instant salvation. Instead, if we would build a solid house in which we may live with some degree of satisfaction and security, we must recognize the importance of our habits, of developing practices and disciplines that will lead to faithful living. We build brick by brick, layer by layer.

Our Christian life is dependent, to a large extent, upon our habits, the practices in our patterns of living that keep our relationship with God-in-Christ strong and vital. In faith, as in life, much is dependent on our habits. In C. S. Lewis's *Screwtape Letters*, the devil says of a new convert to Christianity, "Unless he changes his habits of life, he won't last!"

We are, we say, "creatures of habit." Habits form a major part of what we do each day, from our morning shower to our bedtime snack. If someone ties your hands together with a piece of string, you can break it easily. But if they wrap the string around your wrists many times, you can't break free. Habits, once formed, are not easy to break. It's important in our living to form good habits.

This is especially important for teenagers to remember. In those early and formative years of our lives we are forming habits that will rule our living for the rest of our days. Remember the sign on the country road; "Choose your rut carefully. You will be in it for the next twenty miles."

Jesus said, "Come to me, all you that are weary and are carrying heavy burdens, and I will give you rest. Take my yoke upon you, and learn from me; for I am gentle and humble in heart, and you will find rest for your souls. For my yoke is easy, and my burden is light" (Matthew 11:28–30). I remember, as a young boy, seeing a team of oxen working together in a yoke. It was a rather cumbersome wooden apparatus, but it kept the oxen hauling together, binding them together as a team.

There are certain habits of life that bind us to God and allow us to live and work with Christ as our yoke-fellow. There are things that help us maintain a relationship with him, a sense of his presence, and the confidence of his grace.

So important are these practices that they have been called in Christian tradition "the means of grace." I find the term problematic, because it sounds like these are "means" by which we obtain God's grace—as though grace were something like gasoline and the church a spiritual gas station: so much prayer equals so many gallons of grace.

God's grace is for us, whether we do anything about it or not. It is the way God is, not something he dishes out in dribs and drabs. But there are certain things that we can do, practices or habits that we develop in our lives that can help make our faith strong and keep us close to the One we know in Christ.

What are these habits? The church, especially in its Protestant and evangelical traditions, has emphasized three: the reading and study of the Bible; worship and the sacraments; and prayer—our conversation with God. However, basic to and behind these three, there is a need, a necessity, to recognize the God who addresses us in Jesus Christ in "the Word of God." Even before they were called "Christians," the followers of Jesus were known as "followers of the Way" (Acts 9:2; 11:26; 19:9, 23; 24:22). They understood walking in "the Way" to be based in the Word of God. Followers of Jesus even today who seek to walk in the way must walk in the Word, day by day, year by year.

Eugene Peterson resists the term "spiritual direction" when referring to those habits and disciplines supposed to make the spiritual real. So often they seem to be attempts to manipulate the Spirit rather than an openness to be formed by the Spirit.[5] Rather, he emphasizes that through the Word of God, we seek to be formed by the Spirit of God. Word and Spirit are the manifestation of the same Person-God known to us in Jesus.

Most guides to spiritual reality consist of techniques of self-discipline, meditation, or mystification. They give us steps or rungs by which we may climb the long and intensely vertical ladder to God. I've never had the knees for these. I gravitate toward an understanding of spirituality that is more personal than technological. It seeks its basis in a personal relationship rather than spiritual techniques. "Anything formulaic or technological contributes to a consumer approach to the spiritual life, and we must be on guard against it," warns Peterson. "So easily 'spirituality' becomes a cafeteria through which we walk making selections according to our taste and appetite."[6] The approach I suggest does not pretend to be exciting and entertaining, though it can be both of these. It does not suggest immediate or spectacular results, but rather simple, straightforward habits of faith that over years of living will be both practical and effective.

I don't mean to imply that there is no place or reason for various spiritual disciplines and practices, Christian or other. But I do want to claim, as vigorously as I can, that a specifically Christian spirituality must be based on the Bible, the Word of God.

A faith that is based on the Word of God will consist of receiving and responding—hearing the Word of God and responding in prayer, worship and then walking in the Way, incarnating, living out our faith in our everyday living, both by word and deed.

The word "character" comes from the Greek word meaning to sharpen, cut or engrave, ". . . hence was applied metaphorically to the particular impress or stamp which marked one thing as different from another—its character."[7] A relationship with God, based on the Word of God, if practiced with reverence and devotion, persistence and openness, will produce a character that possesses both grace and strength and as well a deep sense of peace that does indeed pass all understanding and which comes only through faith. In a time when the Bible is considered either a secondary source of spiritual reality or else an infallible account of literal science or history, habits of faith based on the Bible as the Word of God will make a radical difference.

7

RESPONDING TO THE WORD

Participating in the Relationship

"Ho, everyone who thirsts, come to the waters; and you that have no money, come, buy and eat! Come, buy wine and milk without money and without price. Why do you spend your money for that which is not bread, and your labor for that which does not satisfy? Listen carefully to me, and eat what is good, and delight yourselves in rich food."

Isaiah 55:1–2

Habits of faith are practices that strengthen our relationship with God and our life in Christ. They are those practices not enjoined or commanded, but which have grown out of the experiences of people of faith over many years. Chiefly, though not exclusively, they are prayer, worship, and the sacraments, and the reading and study of the Bible.

Why Read the Bible?

Reading the Bible is a bit different from prayer and worship, for the Bible is first of all God's Word to us. The Bible, we have said, is not merely a natural human product. It is inspired by the Spirit of God, not in any literal sense, but as the Spirit reached out to humanity and prophets and apostles responded by telling their part in the grand narrative, the story of God's dealings with his people. However, the reading and study of the Bible are also part of our response to God's Word. The Bible is the Word that we seek to hear, and reading and studying the Bible is our first line of response to the Word.

There are a number of good reasons for anyone to read the Bible, especially anyone who seeks to understand Western culture. The laws and literature, the art and the common customs of all those nations who have been the product of Christendom are saturated with stories, scenes, words, and teachings from the Bible. We need knowledge of the Bible to understand who we are and why we do the things we do. Ours is a culture bred and nurtured by the Bible.

The Bible has influenced Western government and law. For instance, in the British traditions, those who govern are called "ministers"—servants. The "first minister" is called the "prime minister." English Common Law has its foundation in the document called the *Magna Carta,* the "Great Charter." Through the initiative of Stephen Langton, Archbishop of Canterbury at the time, the lords of England met at Ronimede in 1215 and forced King John to sign this document giving at least the lords, if not the common people, certain rights based on law. The first article deals with the freedom of the church.

The language and cadences of the King James Bible of 1611 influenced writers from Milton to John Steinbeck and Ernest Hemingway (many of Steinbeck's and Hemingway's titles are phrases quoted directly from the King James Version Bible). Northrop Frye claimed that one couldn't understand the literature of Western culture without a knowledge of the Bible. He called it "the Great Code." "A student of English literature who does not know the Bible does not understand a good deal of what is going on in what he reads," he wrote.[1]

Though its influence has declined, the Bible continues to be part of the West's common customs and language, and its stories and epics still capture the popular imagination in literature and film. Its content has given rise to our most popular public holidays. However, the primary reason to read the Bible is not for cultural literacy, but for faith, to make firm and enduring our trust in God: "These are written so that you may come to believe that Jesus is the Messiah, the Son of God, and that through believing you may have life in his name" (John 20:31).

The Bible is important to Christian faith so that we may come to believe in Jesus as the Messiah (Christ), and by believing may find life in Christ. Prophets and apostles, ancient scholars, writers and editors, have recorded the story of God's search for a lost and wandering humanity, a humanity that seems to get it wrong continually. Their witness comes to focus in Jesus of Nazareth. The Bible tells us of God's love in Jesus, the One we call "the incarnate Word of God" (John 1:14). The Bible tells us the grand narrative from creation to consummation, and in Jesus we see the very person of God. The Bible is like a window through which we can look upon the Divine, see and understand why we are created, and catch the vision of our eternal home. Through the Bible we can look into the heart of God. *The Bible shows us Jesus, who shows us God.* It is through Jesus Christ our Lord that we know the heart of God and God's love for us.

We do not know the Person or the heart of God through religion or reason. The God of the Bible is not the God we search for and find, but rather the One who finds us. Neither reason nor religion knows God in a personal sense. The God of the Bible is the One who comes looking for us, the lost sheep, the lost children. This is the One "who so loved the world" that he came to seek and to save the lost. In the Bible, through Jesus Christ, we know the person of God as nowhere else in human knowledge and experience.

Then, understood in faith as where we meet God and come to know the grace of God, the Bible proves to be a source of comfort and guidance. The word "comfort" comes from the Latin *con fortes*, meaning "with strength." The Bible gives us strength for living. It steadies us in rough times, like the strap in the subway to hold onto while you're standing and the train is swaying. It provides that extra strength that, when you have stood all you can stand, helps you to still stand (Ephesians 6:11).

People down through the centuries have found strength and even peace in the words of Scripture. So many times, conducting a funeral service, I myself have been deeply moved and comforted by the power and relevance of these ancient words: "The Lord is my shepherd . . ." (Psalm 23:1); "Do not let your hearts be troubled. Believe in God, believe also in me . . ."(John 14:1); or "God is our refuge and strength . . . " (Psalm 46:1). A man in one of my congregations, suffering from depression, memorized and kept repeating the following verse to bring him comfort and strength: "Thou wilt keep him in perfect peace, whose mind is stayed on thee: because he trusteth in thee" (Isaiah 26:3 KJV). Learning and memorizing passages can provide hope, strength, and even peace in times of trial.

The Bible gives us a sense of guidance concerning God's will. "Your Word is a lamp to my feet and a light to my path" (Psalm 119:105). This is not to say, as some have claimed, that the Bible is a roadmap that directs our every move. Some people use the Bible in a random way to get guidance. They close their eyes, open the Bible, and place their finger on a particular spot in the Bible. The verse their finger points to will, they believe, give them the specific guidance they need. This is little more than superstition. There's an anecdote of a person who did just this and read, "[Judas] went and hanged himself" (Matthew 27:5). Thinking there must be a mistake, the person tried again and read, "Go and do likewise" (Luke 10:37)!

There are times when the Bible tells us things we don't like to hear. What T. S. Eliot wrote of the church is true of the Bible:

> Why should men love the Church? Why should they love her laws?
> She tells them of Life and Death, and of all that they would forget.
> She is tender where they would be hard, and hard where they would
> like to be soft.
> She tells them of Evil and Sin, and other unpleasant facts.[2]

"I know the Bible is the Word of God," one woman told me, "because when I read it, it reads me."

During World War II, Bishop Eivind Berggrav was a leader of the resistance in Norway during the Nazi occupation. On the first Sunday of 1942, while a prisoner of the Nazis, the bishop was allowed to write a letter to his wife. He wrote, "He has sent me to heal the broken-hearted, to preach deliverance to the captives, . . . to set at liberty those who are oppressed" (Isaiah 61:1).The letter was censored by the Nazi commandant in Oslo who said to the bishop's wife, "I order you to write to your husband and tell him from now on, he is forbidden to quote the Bible. It is much too up-to-date!"

Because we have assumed that the Bible is to be understood as a history or a science book, to be understood in terms of modernity rather than on its own terms and in its own language, the Bible has ceased to be the Word of God in our time. The result is a culture that is traditionally Christian in name, but is increasingly estranged from its heritage.

There was a time when I would go into a hospital to visit members of my congregation and would be given a file in which people were classified by religion. It was assumed that everyone had a religion, which was assumed to be Christian religion. When admitted into the hospital and asked their religion, people would respond with the denomination with which they were more or less affiliated. Today it can no longer be assumed that anyone has a religion (in the traditional, formal sense) and the question is not asked—at least not where I come from.

Today there are increasing numbers of people who have no "Christian memory." They have no experience in the life and worship of any church nor any knowledge of the Bible. Recently in a Bible study group, I talked of Adam and Eve, and Abraham and Sarah. One bright, young woman, new to our congregation, interrupted me, "I have no idea what you're talking about!"

Her honesty was refreshing, but she's not alone. The fact is that many people who claim the name of Christ, and perhaps are attending a church of their choice every Sunday, have little or no knowledge of the Bible.

The Bible is not a book for casual reading. Listening for the Word of God demands of us openness, concentration, thought, and prayer. As *The Book of Common Prayer*[3] exhorts, we must "read, mark, learn and inwardly digest." We must absorb and be absorbed by the Word of God—Eugene Peterson urges us, "eat this book":

Christians feed on Scripture. Holy Scripture nurtures the Holy Community as food nurtures the human body. Christians don't simply learn or study or use Scripture; we assimilate it, take it into our lives in such a way that it gets metabolized into acts of love,

cups of cold water, mission into all the world, healing and evangelism and justice in Jesus' name, and hands raised in adoration of
the Father.[4]

Prayer: Our Most Personal Response

Prayer is our way of saying "yes" to a relationship with God
in the most personal way. It is communication—a conversation.
It is not a matter of proper words and phrases restricted to certain times and places. It is as natural as a child talking to a loving parent. Formal speech is not required. The lisps and babytalk
of the small child are precious to a parent's ears. Even the talking
is not necessary, for prayer, at its deepest level, is simply the consciousness of God's presence, a communion with God.

Most people pray some time. Even those who claim they don't
believe in God will, in their distress, utter a cry to "something out
there." "There are no atheists in foxholes," we say.

But for many people prayer is only the attempt to get something out of God. They pray because they want something—like
the little girl who, when asked if she said her prayers every night,
responded, "No, 'cos there's some nights I don't want nothin'."

For these people, prayer is essentially pagan. It's like a fire
alarm, a box marked "For use in emergency only." When there's
an emergency, they break the glass, pull the lever, and wait for the
screaming sirens, the red trucks, and the men in yellow raincoats
to swarm all over the place with hoses and axes to put out the
fire. With their first "Our Father" they expect heavenly trumpets
to sound and angels to appear to get them out of the mess they
got themselves into.

Is this all prayer is—merely a way of getting what we want?

If so, the idea of it is not for God's will to be done, but for
my will to be done. In this case, unanswered prayer becomes a
critical problem. We presume that God must never say no,
because God is there to say yes—especially if the request is for
something that seems in accordance with our understanding of
God's character.

But "no" is a valid answer to prayer. Thankfully there are times
when God does say "no." We say God is our heavenly Father. Did
you, father or mother, ever say "no" to your child? Of course you

have—the fire, the razor blade, the piece of glittering glass on the sidewalk. So also God says "no."

What if God always said "yes"? There would be chaos. Imagine if we could order the weather we wanted simply by bending a knee—farmers wanting rain, or vacationers wanting sun. If we can't control our world, even our own lives, what would happen if any fool could order or disorder the universe simply by sending out a few words to the Almighty?

This kind of prayer makes God into no more than an errand boy or a heavenly servant. God would no longer be "Lord." We would be God, and as pagans and sinners that's exactly what we want, to "be like God" (Genesis 3:5)—and this, you may remember, was the sin of Adam and Eve. Fortunately that's what God continually refuses to allow.

There is a difference between the natural prayer of the human heart crying out in distress and the prayer of faith that is in response to the Word of God. Christian prayer is a response to the Word of God. It seeks God's will, not our own.

"Not what I want but what you want," Jesus prayed in Gethsemane (Matthew 26:39; Mark 14:36). That must be our prayer too, "through Jesus Christ our Lord." Praying for what we want is part of prayer. We are still children tugging at God's coat sleeve saying, "Don't forget that I'm here." But it's only a small part. *The purpose of prayer is not to get what we want from God. That's magic. The purpose of prayer is that God may get what he wants from us. That's faith.*

A woman was visiting a friend. As they sat and talked, one of the friend's children came in, a dark-haired little boy about eleven years old. He wanted some candy. His mother said, "No, you've already had enough candy for today."

Then came a rather studious girl about twelve years old. She had a problem with her homework. The mother didn't give her the answer but showed her where she was going wrong.

Next came a little male tornado of nine years, crying with a scraped knee. The mother washed it and kissed it, and miraculously it was made well.

Finally came a quiet little girl about five years old, tugging at her mother's skirt. By this time, the mother was getting a little impatient, so she turned to her and said, "Well, dear, what do you want?" The child replied, "I don't want anything, Mummy, I just want to sit on your knee."

That's prayer at its best, just the sense of being in God's presence. You don't have to ask for anything. You don't have to talk at all.

Most people in this busy age don't realize how wonderful this kind of prayer can be in their lives. It can add a whole new dimension to living. It can add a wonderful depth to human relationships, as when husband and wife can share a conscious sense of God's presence and together "call on the name of the Lord." In times of marital crises, it can be the first step toward reconciliation and renewal.

The prayer of faith, in response to God's Word, is personal. It's not mechanical nor automatic. In our mechanical age we want to flick a switch and see a light come on, turn a key and have a motor start, put in a coin and get an instant cup of coffee. We expect prayer to be that kind of instant service.

You can't "work" prayer like that. You can't treat it like a mechanical thing to be tested to see if it works. Prayer is essentially personal, like friendship, like love, as when two people get to know each other and come to deeper and deeper levels of understanding, trust, and caring. It's like a good marriage whose meaning, depth, and power develop over the years.

This is one of the most tragic aspects of the life of many people—they do not know the real power of prayer. They are like a child picking out a melody on the piano with one finger. When you're five years old, that's kind of cute, but when you're twenty-five, it looks stupid. Many parents teach their children a prayer to say, but they are not able to teach their children how to pray because they've never learned to pray themselves. They go along the road of life quite carelessly until something happens. Then they cry out to God and expect some sort of immediate, satisfactory answer.

Perhaps you have honestly tried prayer, not merely as an instrument of selfishness, but as an honest attempt at a meaningful relationship with God. But you found no sense of God's presence and it seemed like you were talking to thin air. So you stopped. It didn't seem to make much difference in your life whether you prayed or didn't pray, like the little girl who said, "We haven't said grace in our house for a week now, and nothing's happened—yet."

But again, it's not a matter of feeling, but of faith. I have a suspicion, in my own case, that the emptiness of prayer is not of God but of me. In fact, I have become convinced that there is no more important time to pray than when we think we're not being heard, when we feel we're talking into empty air. There have been times in my own life when I have prayed, prayed earnestly, even desperately, without any real sense of being heard, without any feeling of God's presence or God's guidance. However, looking back later, I realized that these have been times I am most sure that God did hear my prayer, though I didn't know or realize it at the time. It was as though God said to me, "Use your head!"

For instance, one such time was my sense of a call to ministry. I prayed desperately for guidance, for some sense of assurance that this was God's will. God seemed silent. In the end, I said, "Lord, I don't know your will, but this is what I think your will could be. I pray you can use my life in your service." Almost fifty years later, I dare to believe that God was guiding me.

Especially in grief situations, when the whole world seems empty and God seems gone, when we cry out to God and no one seems to hear. It is at such a time that we should and we must pray. "Praying through," they used to call it. "Pray until your nose bleeds," advised nineteenth-century revivalist Charles Grandison Finney.[5] Remember the story of Jacob (Genesis 32), the conniving wretch who cheated his father, his brother, his father-in-law, and perhaps many others? One night, afraid and alone by the Jabbok river, he wrestled with a spiritual presence through the night. In the early morning light, he walked away a wounded man, "limping on his thigh," but inwardly healed and ready to face his judgment. Jacob, "the supplanter," was now Israel, "the one who has striven with God and survived."

This is the reason we pray to God "through Jesus Christ our Lord." In other words, as Jesus is the Word of God, we pray in and through the Word of God. We pray to Almighty God, our heavenly Father, but we pray through Jesus Christ our Lord in the assurance of grace, that God hears our prayer whether we feel it or not. This is the prayer of faith. Perhaps not many of us have the determination to "pray until our nose bleeds," but we can all persevere in prayer in patience and continuing hope. In fact, this is one of the wonders of biblical religion, both Jewish and Christian—because our hope is in God, we persevere in spite of adverse circumstances, even when there would seem to be no grounds left for hope—for our hope is finally not in current circumstances, but in God.

"Lord, teach us to pray," the disciples said to Jesus. And Jesus told them a story (Luke 11:5–10, THE MESSAGE):

> Imagine what would happen if you went to a friend in the middle of night and said, "Friend, lend me three loaves of bread. An old friend traveling through just showed up, and I don't have a thing on hand."
>
> The friend answers from his bed, "Don't bother me. The door's locked; my children are all down for the night; I can't get up to give you anything."
>
> But let me tell you, even if he won't get up because he's a friend, if you stand your ground, knocking and waking all the neighbors, he'll finally get up and get you whatever you need.
>
> Here's what I'm saying: Ask and you'll get; Seek and you'll find; Knock and the door will open.

The meaning of the Greek is a kind of persistent imperative: Keep on asking until you receive! Keep on seeking until you find! Keep on knocking, though your knuckles are bloody and sore. For the door will be opened.

> If your little boy asks for a serving of fish, do you scare him with a live snake on his plate? If your little girl asks for an egg, do you trick her with a spider? As bad as you are, you wouldn't think of such a thing—you're at least decent to your own children. And don't you think the Father who conceived you in love will give the Holy Spirit when you ask him?
>
> Luke 11:1–13 THE MESSAGE

Isn't this what we must ask of God, for God's Spirit, for God's Self? Simply to know by faith that God is with us is the essential thing.

Walter Rauschenbusch, known for his advocacy of "the social gospel" in the early days of the twentieth century, tells us something of his own prayer-life, a devotional side not always acknowledged by his critics:

In the castle of my soul is a little postern gate,
Whereat, when I enter, I am in the presence of God.
In a moment, in the turning of a thought,
I am where God is. This is a fact.
When I enter into God, all life has a meaning,
Without asking I know; my desires are even now fulfilled,
My fever is gone in the great quiet of God.
My troubles are but pebbles on the road,
My joys are like the everlasting hills.
So it is when my soul steps through the postern gate
Into the presence of God.
Big things become small, and small things become great.
The near becomes far, and the future is near.
The lowly and despised is shot through with glory. . . .
God is the substance of all revolutions;
When I am in Him, I am in the Kingdom of God,
And in the Fatherland of my soul.[6]

Worship: Longing for More

The importance of habits of faith is no less important simply because some people worship only as a habit. In fact, much of our living is habitual. The life of faith is formed from habits. They nurture our faith by solidifying our sense of God's presence and love.

There is a story told of Thomas Arnold, headmaster of Rugby School in England during the nineteenth century. A boy in the school refused to go to chapel. "It doesn't do any good," he told Arnold, "it's only a habit." Arnold didn't argue, he simply pointed to a wicker wastebasket beside his desk and told the boy to go fill the basket with water. The boy protested that the water would leak out before he got back. "Yes," Arnold agreed, "but think how clean you'll get the basket."

Worship is habitual, week by week, month by month, year by year. We come back again and again to hear God's Word, to know that our lives are cleansed of sin by the forgiveness of God, to set our sights again on the distant goal, to seek the power to become more than we have been, to begin life again in the Spirit of Jesus our Lord. There is a telling phrase in the story of Jesus' return to his hometown. He had just come from an extended period in the desert—that time of spiritual searching, fasting, and prayer that we call "the temptations." He returned to his hometown, Nazareth. When the Sabbath came, he went to the synagogue, "as was his custom" (Luke 4:16–30). In this one little phrase we get an intimate picture of Jesus' lifestyle. For him, worship was a regular part of his life—a habit.

We need fellowship with others who are seeking to live by faith, because we need to know that we are not alone. For this reason, I believe in the importance of corporate worship in our living— the importance of our participation in the worship of the community of faith.

The Greek word for church in the New Testament is *ekklesia.* The church is the *ekklesia,* the "called out." It is comprised of those who have heard God's call to life in Christ, who have heard the Word of God and have responded.

> The Church, the *ekklesia,* is a body of people, not so much assembling because they have chosen to come together, but assembling because God has called them to Himself; not so much assembling to share their own thoughts and opinions, but assembling to listen to the voice of God.[7]

When I go to church on Sunday morning and find people there, I believe in God. I find my own faith strengthened. Why else would people be at church except that God has called them? There are many other things to do on Sunday morning, things many consider more desirable and enticing—outdoor activities, a leisurely breakfast with a cup of coffee and the Sunday paper, or just sleeping in. There is really little sense in trying to convince someone to attend church on a regular basis unless the person has heard God's call and is seeking to respond to God.

If people are seriously trying to live the Christian life, they will go to church out of a desire and need to strengthen their faith through worship and the hearing of God's Word. If people are not living with a sense of God's presence and seeking to do God's will through the rest of the week, it really doesn't matter much whether they go to church or not. It's going to be quite irrelevant to their living.

"Nominal Christianity" is dead. We're either in or we're out. If we mean it, we know that we need all the help we can get. We need the support of a community of faith. We need to join with God's people in hearing and sharing the Word of God. We need to express our sense of gratitude for our lives, gratitude overflowing into praise. And as we receive from others' presence, we offer to them our presence and our faith.

I don't believe there can be solitary Christians. To be a Christian means to be a part of a body, the body of Christ, and that means being an active part of a Christian community.

There's a story told of Charles Spurgeon, a great English preacher at the end of the nineteenth century. One evening he was visiting a man who defined himself as a "solitary Christian." He said to Spurgeon, "I believe in God, but I don't go to church, and I don't believe I need to go to church. Don't you think, Mr. Spurgeon, that a person can be a Christian without going to church?"

In answer, Spurgeon reached down and took a pair of tongs from the fireplace in front of them. Using the tongs, he took one of the coals from the fire and lifted it to the hearth by itself. Then the two men sat in silence and watched the rest of the fire continue to burn brightly while the one coal, sitting by itself, slowly turned cold and black.

Paul Scherer writes,

> We go to church week after week to say to one another, "The goodness of God endureth forever!" And we bow our heads as a sign of God's coming among us. And about it all, to enrich our being here, about the hymns we sing and the prayers our lips form, is the wealth of ten thousand years: poor blind folk of the dim past kneeling before their cruel gods; austere folk marching highly out of Egypt toward the desert and the east; then one day a gentle youth at a carpenter's bench, and such words as never yet man spake; a bitter hour on Calvary, a breathless moment in a garden; and then the long years with their thin red line of martyrs; the gaunt faith of scholar and monk—all this, with the sound of their muffled voices, to enrich our being here—voices that keep with ours chanting, Holy, Holy, Holy, Lord God of hosts!
>
> I believe that when a people turn their backs on that, on these places and these hours which seem to shine with all the light of sacred story—I believe that then . . . there is nothing left on earth that is worth the pain of living! I believe that worship does something that nothing else can do. It satisfies as nothing else, it cleanses as nothing else, it frees us from ourselves, and knits up the broken

fragments of our lives and lifts our faces undaunted again to the hills![8]

When we are talking about worship, we are *not* talking just about words. When the Protestant Reformers spoke of the Word of God, they understood it in the biblical sense of the work of God's Spirit in redemption. However, in reaction to the sacramentalism of the medieval church, the Reformers placed emphasis on preaching. The Word became associated with the words of the preacher with the result that the Protestant/evangelical tradition has tended to neglect the sacraments.

But as the sermon seeks to help us to faith by the spoken word, so the sacraments seek to do the same in a dramatic form. They are, if you will, the picture of the promises of God, an "outward sign," a "visible form."[9] The very physical material of the sacraments assists people who long to touch the invisible God. The sacraments are a way in which people touch and are touched by God in a physical way. They are, for many people, a means of hanging in there when life seems empty and God seems gone. Note for instance, in poet Luci Shaw's story of her grief over her husband's sickness and death, how important to her was the bread and the cup, something she could take in her hand and feel "the bread and wine pressing a tender consciousness of Christ's enfleshment in my heart."[10]

Of course worship is not merely a matter of going to church every now and then as we feel like it. What makes the difference over the years, in our lives and even in the lives of our children and our grandchildren, is the steady regular habit of worship, sharing with the people of God in worship—hearing the Word of God read and preached, participating in the sacraments, raising our prayer and praise in the indefinable longing for something better, something more, which is the very heart of worship.

In Peter Shaffer's play, *Equus,* a psychotic boy who worships horses is in a center for psychiatric treatment. In the course of his treatment, his psychiatrist, a doctor named Dysart, realizes that this deranged boy possesses something that is missing in the doctor's own life.

This psychotic boy would take a particular horse out at night and ride it bareback across the fields, the boy himself naked. He rode fiercely and in ecstasy, exulting in the strength and beauty

of the beast. The psychiatrist realized that in his own dry, analytic life, he knew no such passion nor ecstasy. He commented, "Without worship we shrink! . . . It's as brutal as that!"[11]
As the play begins, the psychiatrist says,

> I keep thinking about the horse! Not the boy, but the horse, and what it may be trying to do. I keep seeing that huge head with its chained mouth. Nudging through the metal some desire absolutely irrelevant to filling its belly or propagating its own kind. What desire could that be? Not to stay a horse any longer? Not to remain reined up forever in those particular genetic strings? . . .
> The thing is, I'm desperate. You see, I'm wearing that horse's head myself. That's the feeling. All reined up in old language and old assumptions, straining to jump clean-hoofed onto a whole new track of being I only suspect is there. I can't see it, because my educated average head is being held at the wrong angle. I can't jump because the bit forbids it, and my own basic force—my horsepower, if you like—is too little![12]

Worship is essential to our humanity because it gives us insight into who we are and why we are here. But more, it gives power to that yearning within us to be more than we are, to be what we are not yet but yet may be, that which we may become by God's grace.

It seems that it is humanity alone among God's creation that is able to worship, to admire and adore and to imitate that which we yearn to be. The object of our admiration has an effect on our living—we tend to become like that which we worship. What we worship decides what we do now and what we shall become.

Michael Polanyi, in his book *Personal Knowledge*, ends more than four hundred pages of reasoned scientific argument by saying:

> So far as we know, the tiny fragments of the universe embodied in man are the only centres of thought and responsibility in the visible world. If that be so, the appearance of the human mind has been so far the ultimate stage in the awakening of the world, and all that has gone before . . . seem to have all been pursuing, along rival lines, the aim now achieved by us up to this point. They are all akin to us. For all these centres . . . may be seen engaged in the same endeavour towards ultimate liberation. We may envisage then a cosmic field which called forth all these centres by offering

them a short-lived, limited, hazardous opportunity for making
some progress of their own towards an unthinkable consummation. And this is also, I believe, how a Christian is placed when
worshipping God.[13]
      . . . Look to the unknown! By these ritual acts the worshipper
accepts the obligation to achieve what he knows to be beyond his
own unaided powers and strives towards it in the hope of a merciful visitation from above.[14]

Those who acknowledge the name of Jesus Christ worship
God as known to us in Jesus. We see in his life, in his love, what
we could be. Through our worship we seek to become more and
more like him, believing that in him we see the fulfillment of our
humanity, and in his teaching the vision of what the kingdom of
God is like. Therefore, the apostle Paul challenges us, "I appeal
to you therefore, brothers and sisters, by the mercies of God, to
present your bodies as a living sacrifice . . . your spiritual worship" (Romans 12:1).

8

BREATHING IN, BREATHING OUT

The Fruit of a Deepening Relationship

> "Go and tell John what you have seen and heard: the blind receive their sight, the lame walk, the lepers are cleansed, the deaf hear, the dead are raised, the poor have good news brought to them."
>
> Luke 7:22

I play the trombone—not very well, but it's a happy hobby. In playing the trombone, or any wind instrument, it is necessary to get enough breath to play the whole musical passage or phrase. Unless I breathe in, there can be neither sound nor music. But of course, unless I blow by breathing out, there isn't any sound either.

So it is with life lived in the Spirit of God. Unless we breathe in the Word of God by the Spirit of God, we don't have the capacity to live the life God calls us to live. And unless we blow, we can't make the music that God is listening for.

When electricians wire a new house, they put in a number of outlets so that electric power can be distributed to the entire house. When manufacturers begin to make a new product, they are care-

ful to arrange for wholesale and retail outlets for effective distri-
bution and sale of the product.

Lakes, too, need outlets if they are to remain clear and clean
and to provide irrigation for the lands around them. The Jordan
river empties into the lowest lying inland basin on earth and runs
into a huge inland lake that has no outlet. The water evaporates
in the intense oven-like heat of the area. The waters of this lake
are thick and salty and the shores of the lake are coated with so
much salt and other minerals that nothing will grow in the area.
This lake is called the Dead Sea.

The life of faith needs outlets as well. We respond to the Word
of God through Scripture, prayer, and worship. The habitual and
continual use of these means of grace may support our faith. But
if faith is to grow strong and vital in our living, it too must have
outlets. The expression of our faith, both in word and deed in our
everyday living, is as important to the life of faith as any of the
others. The Spirit of God is the breath of life. But we can't keep
breathing in unless we also breathe out.

Many people feel that they are not experiencing the fullness of
faith even though they attend church regularly and exercise regularly those habits of faith we have mentioned. It's a good guess
that their faith is simply too anonymous. Their faith is a private
thing. They may live good, respectable lives, but they never con-
fess their faith. They never talk about their faith with others. The
orientation of their living is not service. They never extend themselves to their limits. Worship and prayer, other than private devo-
tions, are formal matters reserved for their proper time and place.
They breathe in, but because they never blow or breathe out, they
never have the joy of making the music.

Before Jesus left the world, he gave his disciples a command—
"the Great Commission"— "Go into all the world and proclaim
the good news to the whole creation" (Mark16:15). He wasn't
speaking only of Asia and Africa, those places overseas to which
the church has sent missionaries. He was saying, "Go into your
world"—into the office or the kitchen, the store or the classroom
or the factory. It's important for anyone who owns the name of
Jesus to realize that he or she is a missionary.

We often miss the fact that John 3:16 says, "God so loves the
world." It does not say, "God so loves the *church.*" It does not

say even "God so loves *me.*" The world includes us all, unrighteous as well as righteous. God loves all creation, even those who
reject him and who despoil creation and hurt and harm others.
To me, that is truly amazing. But isn't it what the cross is about?

We are "ambassadors of Christ": "in Christ God was reconciling the world to himself, not counting their trespasses against
them, and entrusting the message of reconciliation to us. So we
are ambassadors for Christ, God is making his appeal through
us" (2 Corinthians 5:19–20).

How does the Word of God shape our life in the world? Living in and by the Word in the world is the expression of our faith.
"Faith without works is dead" (James 2:26).

Speaking the Word into the World

The word "evangelism" has become an emotionally loaded
word for many people, even within the church itself. For these
people, it intimates a narrow, bigoted, exclusive, self-righteous
Christianity of which they want no part.

I have been amazed at the negative attitude toward evangelism.
While many people have been helped and lives have been changed,
there can be no doubt that misguided efforts of evangelism have
helped to create a negative attitude toward the Christian faith itself.

Some think immediately of one of those traveling evangelists
who would come into a community, hold a series of meetings, get
the emotionally unstable excited, divide the community over some
point of Christian doctrine, and then leave with a large bundle of
cash they have the audacity to call a "love offering."

Some will remember attending a revival meeting or evangelistic service as a child when a preacher pounded the pulpit, pointed
at people, and shouted about damnation and the tortures of hell.
As a result, for weeks after, they lived in terror of both God and
death. Once when I left the pulpit while preaching and walked
down the aisle among the congregation, a woman near the front
grew very disturbed. When I talked to her later, I learned that
when she was a child her grandmother had taken her to a revival
meeting. The evangelist had come down to where they were sitting and, pointing his finger at her, told her if she didn't accept

Jesus then and there, she would go to hell eternally. "When you came down that aisle," she said, "that horrible experience flashed back before my eyes."

It is healthy to rebel against such false piety and hypocritical religiosity. It is good to reject such unfitting expressions of the gospel. But should we throw the true and essential out with the false, the *evangel* with what we have mistakenly called "evangelism"?

Evangelism is essential to the gospel. It means sharing the "good news." It implies a speaking, a telling, a proclamation. The gospel is its own imperative.

Evangelism demands a speaking. It cannot be anonymous. It forces us to come to grips with not only the social but also the ultimate dimensions of our humanity—our relationship with God.

"Voicing" is what a technician does in tuning a pipe organ. It is not only a matter of tuning the pipe organ, but also of ensuring that each sound is true—that the trumpet sounds like a trumpet and that the reed stops sound like reed instruments. The congregation is a kind of pipe organ that in the hands of a capable technician may give effective and responsible voice to the gospel. The full and faithful life of the local congregation is the most effective means of witness and evangelism in the church today, and this is a methodology that is true to all the traditions of Christ's church.

Evangelism is not a special ministry tacked on to the ordinary life of a congregation. We evangelize whether we realize it or not. Wherever a local congregation exists, evangelism is happening. It may be happening in ways that are ineffective or counterproductive, but it is happening.

Evangelism is taking place when you put up a sign in front of the church with the names of the church and its minister(s) and the timings of Sunday services. When you walk into church on Sunday morning, you're making a statement to those around you in the community. When the sound of the bell or the singing of a hymn sounds across the street, it's a message. Evangelism, in the broadest sense, is whatever the church does to relate the gospel to the world. People may go away untouched by grace, without any sense of God's presence in their lives. But the ordinary life of the church, especially through what we have traditionally called "the means of grace" (and which I have called "habits of faith"), can in every moment of its contact with people of the world be an effective evangelistic opportunity.

In this sense then, every member of the church has the opportunity and the responsibility to be an evangelist. In the life of the church and the work of the gospel we are all responsible participants, not passive recipients, witnesses rather than spectators.

This is why I would claim that the most effective and responsible method of evangelism for the church today is through the local congregation—in its worship *(litourgia)*, its preaching *(kerygma)*, its fellowship *(koinonia)*, and its service to others *(diakonia)*.

Litourgia, the Greek word for "liturgy," refers to the form and content of our worship. Originally it meant an act of voluntary service to the community or state. *Kerygma* is the word for the gospel message, the preaching of the apostles. *Koinonia* refers to the fellowship among the people of the church: "Behold how they love one another!" *Diakonia* is the service rendered to others in Christian love.

The first thing, then, is that we be conscious of who we are and what we are doing, both corporately and individually. We are not consumers of religion but coworkers in the kingdom of God. This requires a whole different mindset—not that of preserving the ecclesiastical institution, but of serving the *oecumenos,* the world God loves in the name and grace of Jesus Christ. That last phrase is essential for the church. It identifies why we do what we do, all in the name and the grace of Jesus Christ.

This seems a difficult concept to realize, not because it's so complicated but because it's so different. Generally our attitude in the life of the local congregation is to get people in so that there are more to share the load, particularly the financial load. Whenever we speak of outreach or evangelism, we plan programs to bring people in. Soon these programs become tainted with a concern for the institution, the church, rather than for the individual and for God's world. But church growth is not synonymous with evangelism. When people used to speak of "the love of souls," this is what they meant—a concern for the welfare of the "souls," the people, whom God loves.

Evangelism is rooted in relationship, not technique. The revivalist methodology, effective as it was, left a lot to be desired in this regard. It tended to be mechanical. As I mentioned in an earlier chapter, Charles Grandison Finney, the father of revivalism, developed techniques, which he called "methods" or "means," to ensure revival. "Promoting a revival of religion [ought] to be judged by the ordinary rules of cause and effect," wrote Finney.[1]

The "means" that Finney developed were adapted and perfected, and in fact became in a general sense a means of manipulation.[2] The emphasis upon means and methods resulted in the development of a procession of specialist evangelists who would come into a community, spin a well-worn record of predigested sermons, call for commitments, and then leave the local clergy to deal with both follow-up and let-down.

However, there is a place for responsible evangelistic methodology, like that of Billy Graham and Dwight L. Moody. We should never disparage the contribution they have made to the church and to the cause of Christ. But even Graham and Moody have admitted that their work did little to touch people outside the Christian fellowship.

There has been, until recent years, a preoccupation with the soul and a lack of concern for the physical condition. It was assumed that the physical condition would improve once the spiritual condition was rectified. Since "the great reversal"[3] at the close of the nineteenth century, the evangelical tradition closed in upon itself with little care for the reform and welfare of the world around it. It has shown little concern for the criticism and correction of those social systems and conditions that oppressed those caught in their mesh and gave them little opportunity for any kind of meaningful liberation or salvation.

Because evangelism has been understood in terms of mechanistic techniques, it has often shown little responsibility for the results of its efforts. Converts have been left to find their own way into the fellowship of a local church where they might be nurtured and find some understanding of what has happened to them. "The new birth gives potential for personality change, but the change does not take place automatically. Conversion must lead to Christian growth," wrote Leighton Ford.[4] Ford, brother-in-law of Billy Graham and himself a noted evangelist, introduced a strong social concern in the development of his evangelism, training churches to respond to social needs identified in the local community.[5]

Recognition of social needs helps temper the triumphal tone of some evangelism. In the light of current and recent social history, we must show a fair measure of humility. As Christians cannot point to themselves, but only beyond themselves to the gospel, so the church cannot ultimately point to itself, but to its Lord. Sadly, some Christians have never realized that conquest is no longer a proper means of converting people to the kingdom of God. Some still see Christian evangelism in terms of a spiritual "crusade"—going forth to conquer (albeit spiritually) in the name of Christ. They define victory by numbering the converts and crediting their program. But our Lord is not a conquering hero riding in triumph on a horse, but the One who came to serve and to save, riding humbly on a donkey to the place of his final sacrifice.

Because we who are the church fall short of what we are called to be, we cannot simply identify the church with the truth, let alone the Word. We can point only to where the Spirit of Christ is revealed, where the rule of God is made plain in the world. As Barth observed:

> The only advantage of the Church over against the world is that the Church knows the real situation of the world. Christians know what non-Christians do not. . . . It belongs to the Church to witness to the Dominion of Christ clearly, explicitly, and consciously.[6]

Since the church's function is that of witness, it can never claim authority independent of grace. It cannot validate or consolidate the truth or power of the gospel in itself. It is too often itself a denial of the gospel it professes!

Therefore, other than its faith, its knowledge of and trust in God's grace, the church cannot claim to have something that the rest of the world does not have, or claim to be something that the rest of the world is not. Faith is no small thing, and it does change lives. But, as we have insisted, faith is neither our possession nor that of the church—it is a gift of God. So the church can only point to the grace it knows—the grace of Jesus Christ, which is free and unconditional.

We often fail to distinguish between "free" and "cheap." If an article is free, if it doesn't cost anything, we think it must be worthless. But that is not necessarily so—love has no bargain-basement prices. If it has a price tag attached, it is prostitution. True love is given freely, but not cheaply. One who loves is willing to give at great cost: "For God so loved the world that he gave his only Son . . ." (John 3:16).

There is a difference between free grace and cheap grace. The Protestant Reformers affirmed that God's grace is free to all who believe, but since then the Protestant churches have often made it cheap instead of free. Cheap grace is like getting the answer without doing the math, attending church on Sunday without the life of discipleship the rest of the week. Twentieth century theologian and Christian martyr Dietrich Bonhoeffer discerned the difference:

> Cheap grace is the preaching of forgiveness without requiring repentance, baptism without church disciplines, communion without confession, absolution without contrition. Cheap grace is grace without discipleship, grace without the cross, grace without Jesus Christ, living and incarnate.[7]

Free grace is costly because it cost God the life of his Son, and a genuine response to such sacrificial love demands a wholehearted response.

While a Christian cannot claim righteousness in himself or herself, the fruit of a wholehearted relationship to God manifests itself in all of life: not simply in the truth to which we point, but in the truth of how we live. The church has too often divorced evangelism from service.

In the early church, the words of faith were not separated from the works of love. They went together, word and deed, preaching and healing, teaching but also concern for the poor and the "little ones" (Matthew 18:1–7, 10–11). In Mark the command is to "Go and proclaim" (Mark 16:15); in Matthew to "Go and make disciples . . . and teach" (Matthew 28:19–20); while in Luke and Acts, the disciples are to be "witnesses" (Luke 24:48; Acts 1:8). The disciples of Jesus are not to merely preach and teach; they are to embody the message in their living. Christian witness was both do and tell. It still is.

Living Out the Word: Love of God and Neighbor

My mother had it together. She was a "two-legged Christian" in both word and deed. Some say she was a better preacher than my father, but she was also a nurse, and often in towns where medical facilities were limited or nonexistent she would be called on in an emergency. Once, in later years, I took her back to the place where my father had been a minister when I was born. At one farmhouse, she knocked at the back door. An elderly woman came to the door and peered out through the screen. "Hello, Emma," my mother said. The door flew open and Emma seized mother in her arms. "Mrs. Reynolds!" she cried, tears running down her face.

That was typical of the kind of love people felt for my mother wherever she went. One of her favorite sayings was, "What you do speaks so loudly I can't hear what you say."

The fact is that Jesus gave us both the Great Commission, to go and preach, and the Great Commandment, to love God and one's neighbor. The first is the "telling," to "go and preach the gospel." The second is the "doing," to love God and one's neighbor.

A lawyer came to Jesus with a question: "Which commandment is the first of all?" (Mark 12:28). His question was a natural one for the time. The original simple law, the Ten Commandments, had become overlaid with a multitude of regulations and prescriptions so that almost every common action of the people was regulated by some command or tradition—sacrifices at the temple, what they could or couldn't do on the Sabbath, how much of their grain harvest or how many of their flocks had to be given to the priesthood. Were all these regulations of equal importance, or were some more important than others?

In answering the question, Jesus gave his questioner not one commandment, but two: "The first is, 'Hear, O Israel: the Lord our God, the Lord is one; you shall love the Lord your God with all your heart, and with all your soul, and with all your mind, and with all your strength.' The second is this, 'You shall love your neighbor as yourself.' There is no other commandment greater than these" (Mark 12:30–31).

The answer was one of the most important answers Jesus gave to any question. His answer has become the basis of the ethic of the Christian life—the love and service of God and of neighbor. Too often we tend to separate these commandments. We practice one to the neglect of the other. But Jesus puts them together—and we cannot, must not, tear them apart. Jesus was saying that the love and service of God must never be separated from the love and service of one's neighbor—and that the love and service of others must never be separated from the love and service of God.

Early religions consisted almost entirely of incantations and sacrifices to appease or win the benevolence of some local deity. Only at an advanced stage did most religions begin to consider that human welfare and justice toward others might be part of the deity's concern.

Remember that this "first commandment" was well known to the Hebrew people as the basic creed of Judaism, the *Shema*: "Hear, O Israel: the Lord is our God, the Lord alone. You shall love the Lord your God with all your heart, and with all your soul, and with all your might"(Deuteronomy 6:4–5). The second commandment, to "love your neighbor as yourself," was buried away among the laws of the book of Leviticus (Leviticus 19:18). It was an obscure verse of Scripture, but Jesus put the two commandments together, insisting that they remain together.

This is one of the most unique points of Christian faith. Divine service and human service must be held together. One might even say that the service of God is the service of others. The prophet Amos cried,

> I hate, I despise . . . your solemn assemblies . . . your burnt offerings and grain offerings. . . . Take away from me the noise of your songs; I will not listen to the melody of your harps. But let justice roll down like waters, and righteousness like an ever-flowing stream.
>
> Amos 5:21–24

Jesus related what we have come to call the parable of the last judgment. When the Son of Man shall come in judgment, he shall separate the righteous from the unrighteous, the sheep from the goats. But the basis of his judgment will not be how often we have gone to church, but rather how we have treated our neighbors.

> "Come, you that are blessed of my Father, inherit the kingdom prepared for you from the foundation of the world; for I was hungry and you gave me food, I was thirsty and you gave me something to drink, I was a stranger and you welcomed me, I was naked and you gave me clothing, I was sick and you took care of me, I was in prison and you visited me." Then the the righteous will answer him, "Lord, when was it that we saw you hungry and gave you food, or thirsty and gave you something to drink? And when was it that we saw you a stranger and welcomed you, or naked and gave you clothing? And when was it that we saw you sick or in prison and visted you?" And the king will answer them, "Truly I tell you, just as you did it to one of the least of these who are members of my family, you did it to me."
>
> Matthew 25:31–40

If that's not enough, the writer of the first letter of John says it quite pungently: "Those who say, 'I love God,' and hate their brothers or sisters, are liars" (1 John 4:20).

So today, if we think that God will be pleased by hymns and prayers, a beautiful sanctuary and a fine collection of reasonably respectable people, we're mistaken. The service of God, what pleases the loving heart of the Father, is still the action that supplies the needs of the hungry, the thirsty, the sick, the helpless and the homeless, the lonely, the outcast and the confined.

However, it would seem that since the service of God is the service of the neighbor, therefore the service of the neighbor is the service of God. But this doesn't necessarily follow. We cannot truly serve God apart from the service of our fellow human beings, but this should not lead us to think that we can therefore simply serve others as a substitute for the love and service of God.

This is a day of rebellion against institutionalized religion. Many people of good heart and humanitarian concern equate serving God with supporting good causes and make their service club or volunteer association a substitute for faith and fellowship in the Christian community. They may be commended for their concern for others, and their acts may be done in a spirit of self-giving love. Yet, without recognition of the divine dimension of human service, does not our human love so often run pale and thin?

The love and service of others gives life its horizontal dimension. But the love of God gives life its vertical dimension. Without that vertical dimension, life becomes one dimensional, flat—a Dali landscape, an Eliot wasteland:

> Waste and void. Waste and void.
> And darkness upon the face of the deep![8]

If human beings are seen no longer as children of God, created in the image of God, not as an immortal soul of infinite value in God's sight but only as a chance and passing collection of cellular life, then human service, to me, loses something of its meaning. If we do not see Christ in our neighbor, in "the least of these," then any act of human service loses its eternal significance. It may be a beautiful act of passing kindness, but it is no longer something of eternal consequence because it is not done to the Eternal in us.

But the two commandments taken together form a cross: the vertical dimension consists of the love and service of God, and the horizontal dimension consists of the love and service to one's neighbor. It is this love, not just a transitory act of goodness, but an expression of the Eternal Love, which gives meaning and purpose to the love of the neighbor. It forms the foundation of all human living and striving and is the very heart and soul of the universe.

In addition to noticing that the two commands cannot be separated, we should also notice their specific order. The second commandment, the love and service of the neighbor, is dependent upon and a derivative of the first. The first question of the Shorter Catechism of the Westminster Confession asks, "What is the chief end of man?" and answers, "Man's chief end is to glorify God and to enjoy Him forever." The unique purpose of our humanity is not our own happiness, our own welfare, either individual or collective. When we seek our own happiness, our happiness eludes us. For happiness is the byproduct of our glorifying God. We seek to build the perfect social order, but it is only when we can discover the rule of God that we will indeed discover the kingdom for which we are searching and longing and striving.

On that first Christmas, when the angels sang, their song was first, "Glory to God in the highest!" And then, "Peace on earth, goodwill to all peoples!" We will not have peace and goodwill upon earth until our attempts at the love and service of humanity are coupled with our attempts to love and serve the One whose illimitable Love we see symbolized in the cross.

But this love means a new understanding of holiness.

Holiness: The Evidence of Love

Breathing in and breathing out the Word shapes a life of holiness—not a holiness referring only to our relationship with God, but a holiness that necessarily includes our relationship with others. One cannot be holy to one's self—Jesus and me. The holiness of the Word of God, the holiness we see in the life of Jesus, the holiness to which we are called, is the holiness of love. Love is lived in relationship with others, in the world God loves.

In *The Idea of the Holy,*[9] German writer Rudolf Otto explored this mystery that people so continually seek to deny but which can never be quite completely erased from our consciousness. He called it the *numinous*, and he observed that it can be found in all human cultures.

Otto's work helps identify our sense of something that is always at the edge of our consciousness: the *mysterium tremendum*, the tremendous mystery at the heart of life, what Karl Barth called the *totaliter aliter*, the "wholly Other," the transcendent, the eternal. We may ignore it to some extent. The busyness of living or the pursuit of pleasure may obscure the still, small voice. But then in the holy darkness of a sleepless night, in a moment of loneliness in the midst of a crowded city, when we look in the mirror and really see ourselves, or when in the middle of our common work we find ourselves thinking—again we have that sense of responsibility and possibility, an ideal vision of what we are meant to be and yet are not.

The "numinous" appears a unique way in the Hebrew tradition:

Worship the Lord in the beauty of holiness.
The Lord is in His holy temple; let all the earth keep silence.
'Consecrate yourselves and be holy, for I am holy,' says the Lord.

And it seems to command of us a response. Our first response (if we choose to respond) is to stop and listen. In the presence of the Holy, we look at ourselves and at our lives in the context of eternity, considering what we should be and what we would be. In the wilderness, a bush seemed to burn and was not consumed, and Moses was filled with a sense of the burning presence of the Holy. "Remove the sandals from your feet, for the place on which you are standing is holy ground." In response, Moses, if reluctantly, went back to Egypt to lead his people to freedom (Exodus 3:1–4:18). Isaiah in the temple heard the seraphim singing, "Holy, Holy, Holy, is the Lord of hosts." He responded, "Here am I; send me!" (Isaiah 6:1–10).

The second step, if we choose to respond to the presence of the Holy, is almost automatic. Our response is awe, reverence, and worship. As we gather week by week for worship, we seek to be open to the possibility we may find again that this may be a holy moment, that our hearts may hear the Word of grace and truth, which is not just a human word, the preacher's word, but the Word of God.

Our third step is the effect that our encounter with the Holy will have in our living. With the sense of the Holy comes a sense of who we should be, a sense of "oughtness," a sense of what Kant called "the categorical imperative,"[10] "the moral law within."[11] An encounter with the Holy will make us seek to be more like the Holy.

In the Hebrew, the word for "holy" is *qadhosh*. It comes from a root meaning "to cut, to separate." In Hebrew understanding, and common to human religions, that which is holy is cut off, separated from common usage for sacred purposes.

And still in the Christian church we speak of the holy Bible, or the holy sacraments, or holy baptism, and even the holy church. We consecrate a place for worship that is set apart from common use. We divide life into the sacred and the secular, those things that are "holy" and those things that are common. In traditional terms, the road to holiness was found in turning from the world and things of the world, in taking the path of asceticism, of prayer and contemplation. It is perhaps understandable that, amid the corruption of the late Roman Empire, the early church believed that to achieve holiness it was necessary to cut one's self off from the world, to go to the desert to seek perfection in a life of prayer, or to live with a small group of like-minded people a life of rigorous spiritual discipline.

This is the way the monastic movement began, and some traditions of the Christian church still divide their priesthood into "the secular" who serve the church in parishes (in the world), and "the religious" or "the perfect" who withdraw from the world to a life of contemplation and prayer, a life of holiness.

The Protestant Reformation, with its return to the Scripture, brought a different understanding. The call of God to holiness did not mean withdrawal from the world, but serving God in the world. There were no Protestant monasteries. Much of the ornamentation used to denote the holiness of God was cast off—images and art works in churches, elaborate vestments for the clergy, incense and esoteric practices in the liturgy. The altar, symbolizing the presence of God, was moved from the chancel (from which the people were separated by a wall or a fence) to become the communion table, symbolizing the presence of God in the midst of the people. The elements for the communion service were to be the bread and drink of their common life, and the people were to receive both.

We seem to have two understandings of holiness. The first might be called "the holiness of the Law," attained by means of separation from all that is unclean (a cutting off, as in the Hebrew word *quadhosh*). It means following the guidelines, the customs, the laws that set people apart, separating them from that which is sinful and unclean. It is a righteousness that we might conceivably approximate. By keeping the commandments, even proximately, I can pat myself on the back. "God, I thank you that I am not like other people" (Luke 18:9–14.) But this kind of holiness can maintain itself only by its very rigidity, and so lacks the qualities of mercy, forgiveness, and grace, which Nicholas Berdyaev called "the morality beyond morality,"[12] the necessary corollary of love.

In Jesus Christ we see a second and different kind of holiness. In the New Testament, the understanding of holiness is a holiness of love—not a separation from but an involvement in, not a drawing back from sinners and sinful situations because my purity might be sullied, but a "going into all the world" and being involved in the business of living, in commerce and labor and politics, all in the spirit of holiness.

The holiness of love can be fulfilled only in relationship with God and others. It is a holiness of right relationships, for love is necessarily a relationship. We cannot be righteous in ourselves, no matter how many things we do or do not do. This holiness is dependent upon our relations with others, upon justice and mercy. It is a higher holiness, a righteousness that "exceeds the righteousness of the scribes and Pharisees"—not self-righteousness, but righteousness of relationships.

This is the holiness we see in the life and ministry of Jesus, who was derided as a "friend of publicans and sinners" and denounced as a glutton and a drunkard. He spoke harsh words to those who tried so hard to prove themselves righteous but in their legalism neglected justice and mercy. They would tithe the tiny seeds of herbs, one in ten for God, but they would not help the man who fell among thieves as he lay groaning in the ditch—because such contact might render them impure.

This is the kind of holiness we see in the incarnation—the holiness of God. Too long have we thought of God up in heaven, a God whose holiness must be satisfied if we are ever to be acceptable in his sight. Because God is holy, he cannot get involved in the dirty, sinful things of this world.

But the Bible tells us that "God so loved the world" (John 3:16) that "in Christ God was reconciling the world to himself" (2 Corinthians 5:19). In fact, the very heart of the gospel is that God does get involved:

> Let Christ himself be your example as to what your attitude should be. For he, who had always been God by nature, did not cling to his prerogatives as God's equal, but stripped himself of all privilege by consenting to be a slave by nature and being born as mortal man. And, having become man, he humbled himself by living a life of utter obedience, even to the extent of dying, and the death he died was the death of a common criminal.
>
> Philippians 2:5–8 PHILLIPS

Here is a holiness that shall indeed create in our hearts both awe and fear. It is not the fear of the Israelites who thought they would be destroyed in approaching the holy mountain (Exodus

19:12), but the fear that in being embraced by this holy love and called to such a life of self-giving love, we will lose all that we presently have and are. But, as we shall see in our next chapter, it is only by losing ourselves in this self-giving love that we find the fulfillment of our humanity.

Dag Hammerskjold, a Swedish statesman who became Secretary General of the United Nations, died in 1961 in a plane crash in the Congo on a mission of peace. He left behind a diary revealing the pilgrimage of a deeply religious man.[13] One of his statements is almost shocking in its simplicity—"In our present era, the road to holiness necessarily passes through the world of action."

The call to life in the Spirit of Jesus Christ cannot be a call to leave the world or any part of the world in a self-seeking quest for holiness. Christian holiness is a call to get involved in the world that God loves—that scarred, sinning, corrupt, hurting world that in its anxiety and self-concern has turned from God. It is a call to action, to get involved, and to take risks. It is a call to go into those places where there is hurt and confusion, where there may be immorality and injustice. In the words of George MacLeod of Iona:

> I simply argue that the Cross be raised again at the centre of the market place as well as on the steeple of the Church. I am recovering the claim that Jesus was not crucified in a Cathedral between two candles, but on a cross between two thieves, on the town garbage heap, on a crossroads so cosmopolitan that they had to write His title in Hebrew, Latin and Greek . . .; at the kind of place where cynics talked smut, and thieves cursed, and soldiers gambled. Because that is where He died and that is what He died about, that is where Church people should be and what Church people should be about.[14]

Holiness is shaped within us as we deepen our relationship with the Word of God. It is the evidence of love, because God is love, and when we are in relationship with God we begin to take on God's likeness. The entire Bible points to this love—the kind we know in Jesus Christ, which is the foundation and the expression of the intimacy to which God calls us.

9

THE "WHY" OF RELATIONSHIP

Reading for the Love of God

The two most difficult things to get straight in life are love and God. More often than not, the mess people make of their lives can be traced to failure or stupidity or meanness in one or both of these areas. . . . If we want to deal with God the right way, we have to learn to love the right way. If we want to love the right way, we have to deal with God the right way. God and love can't be separated.

Eugene Peterson[1]

To walk each day in the knowledge and the confidence of God's love, to be empowered to show and give that love to others is ultimately why we seek God in the Bible. It is not in order to master absolute truth (the right facts or the correct doctrine), nor to follow all the rules for personal morality, nor learn techniques for spiritual growth, nor how to distill a manifesto for social action. How tragic it would be to spend a lifetime reading the Bible and miss the opportunity to discover that which we were created for in God's image: a relationship with God and others.

Sometimes the Word of God in the Bible is obscured by human fear, bitterness, or greed, but through the entire grand narrative, from creation to fulfillment, the God, whose Word it is, is inviting us to enter into a relationship with him. It all comes into focus in the love of Jesus. The cross is the very symbol of this love. Here we learn what love is.

The Way to Self-Fulfillment

We talk a lot about self-fulfillment. Guides to it fill the spirituality sections of our bookstores. The trouble is that we are going about it the wrong way. There's a paradox here. Self-fulfillment is like happiness: you don't find it by going after it, because it is a byproduct. You find self-fulfillment not by satisfying your desires, but by giving yourself away in love.

I once asked members of a Bible study and discussion group to recall a time in their lives when they had felt the happiest and most fulfilled.

For one woman, it was teaching a group of music students. The students had been practicing diligently and finally it all came together. It was the sound that she had been hoping for! Her face glowed as she remembered. For another woman, it was standing in the elevator when she was coming home from the hospital with her first child. For one of the men, it was on his wedding day, waiting for his bride to come down the aisle.

All these moments had something in common: these people were so completely involved in what they were doing that they forgot about themselves. This involvement could involve sacrifice, even pain, and it included some sort of responsibility. It was something or someone they loved so much, that meant so much to them and was of such value to them, that the cost was unimportant.

In such moments we feel most alive and fulfilled, even though they are moments of almost complete self-forgetfulness. "For those who want to save their life will lose it, and those who lose their life for my sake will find it" (Matthew 16:25).The Greek word means either "life" or "soul," and is identified closely with what we would call the "self." For my friends in our small group, it was when they were most ready to lose themselves that they found themselves. I think the secret to their experiences was love. They were immersed in what they loved, and love is life-giving. Love is what fulfils us. When Jesus came to live in love among us and to die for us, he showed us that the nature of love is not self-seeking, but self-giving. This is the fulfillment of our faith and the highest expression of our humanity.

Perhaps no word in our language is more misused and misunderstood than the word "love." Popular singers, romance novelists, developmental psychologists, and preachers extol love in a thousand different definitions. The only point of agreement seems to be that love is the fulfillment of our deepest desires and the answer to the riddle of life.

The Love We Define

There are many different kinds of love. The love shared between parents and children, lovers, husbands and wives, close friends, and the love of citizens for their country. The Bible proclaims, "God is love" (1 John 4:8, 16). This one word has many different meanings.

The ancient Greeks used at least four words for love, which seemed to progress across levels of emotional and personal maturity, from the self-centered desire of the infant to the self-giving love of the mother.

Epithymia refers to the physical aspect of love—sexual desire, even lust. The corresponding word in Latin is *libido*, which Sigmund Freud used to signify the basic human sexual drive. *Epithymia* is comparable to the most infantile level of love. The Greeks used it to describe a baby's hunger for its mother's milk.

Love does have its physical side, and this is a good thing. The first chapter of the Bible tells us that when the earth was created, God looked on all that had been made and called it good. And the message of the New Testament is that "the Word became flesh"—that God took on our physical nature. In Jewish and Christian thought, there is no essential evil in physical cravings, not even in sexual desire.

Infants are completely dependent, and therefore completely self-centered. Their thoughts are only for the satisfaction of their needs. Initially they are unable to respond, and can only react. It is several weeks before they can manage a first feeble affective response—a smile. This is the first personal response to parental affection and attention rather than a simple reaction to hunger or pain.

It is natural for infants to be this way. But it is a tragedy when some people fail to grow beyond this level of emotional maturity. Love, for them, continues to be a self-centered thing, largely physical, with little or no sense of commitment or responsibility. When human sexuality is no more than physical, when it is simply selfish, casual, or irresponsible, it is emotionally infantile.

The second word the Greeks used was *eros*. In popular understanding, *eros* has come to mean what *epithymia* meant originally; hence the word "erotic." I would compare this to a second level of emotional maturity, what we might call "teenage love."

For the Greeks, *eros* came to be understood in a spiritual rather than a physical sense, especially in its later development. In its highest Platonic expression, *eros* is the love of the good, the true, and the beautiful. Once again, this desire is not a bad thing in itself. Surely it is good to love and desire goodness, truth, and beauty. But it is a type of love that is still an expression of our desire and is still essentially self-centered.

This love has been called "because love." It is the love of a woman *because* she is beautiful or intelligent, the love of a man *because* he is courageous or strong. It is the love of another *because* of the qualities perceived in that other person. And it is these qualities that cause or create the love.

So this love, which we sometimes call "romantic love," is not something we create or do ourselves. It is something that happens to us. We speak of "falling in love." Here the important thing is not to be loving, but to be desirable, to make yourself as attractive as possible so that others might fall in love with you.[2] This type of love is the grand passion of novels, plays, and movies. This is the adoration of a teenager for a movie star or sports hero. It is the love of Romeo and Juliet (and remember, they were teenagers).

Glorious as this love may sometimes seem, it is still basically a self-centered desire. It is a craving to possess for ourselves the thing we admire—not so much the person we love as the qualities they possess, not who they are so much as what they are.

Therefore they become not some*one* to whom we must relate, but some*thing* we seek to acquire as a possession.

Both *epithymia* and *eros* are actually forms of self-love: physical satisfaction and psychological satisfaction, respectively. This is why romantic love alone, while it may attract two people to each other, is not a sufficiently mature basis for marriage. To find the basis of a mature and lasting relationship, we must go beyond a basically selfish love to a love that is able to respond with care and concern for the other. This is the reason our romantic literature is so filled with tragedy, ending so often in suicide and death.[3] It is why Hollywood, the love capital of the world, can only show an impermanent and immature form of love, serial monogamy, marriages ending in divorce as soon as the passion is gone.

To be able to find permanence and stability in our relationships and to perpetuate a relationship as responsible and permanent as marriage, we need to attain to the next level of maturity in love. *Philia* is the kind of love necessary for any fulfilling and stable relationship. It is usually defined as "brotherly love," but the essential meaning of the word is actually "mutual love." Aristotle called it "love between equals." It is *responsible* love, able to respond to the love of another.

This is the kind of love that is necessary for any permanence and happiness in relationships such as friendship and marriage—a reciprocal love that is both offered and returned. A successful marriage or friendship can never be merely a one-sided affair—one person always giving and the other always receiving. It must be mutual.

Let's be clear that this love is not just a feeling or passion. It's not something that just happens to you or something you fall into. It's the ability to respond to the affection of the other. As Erich Fromm observed, it's an action, something you *do:*

> Love is an activity, not a passive affect; it is a "standing in," not a "falling for." In the most general way, the active character of love can be described by stating that love is primarily *giving*, not receiving.[4]

Those who are happily married will tell you that permanent happiness and love in marriage are not based to any major degree upon the passionate feelings that may have propelled them into marriage in the first place. Enduring happiness and love develop as two people learn to show each other affection and concern, patience and sympathy, kindliness and respect. Without these, the passion of love soon runs out and shows itself to be the self-centered thing it is. And there's nothing so futile as trying to live with a self-centered person who has little concern for anyone else.

It may sound as though this "responsible love" is drudgery. The miracle is that where this love is realized, it can be wonderful, even when it manifests itself in changing diapers and wiping runny noses.

Agape is the *highest* level of development in our ability to grow in love. It is a self-giving love not based in need or desire, nor compelled by qualities of beauty, goodness, or truth in the other, nor extended in expectation of return, response, or reward. It is simply its nature to express itself without interest in or regard for the cost or the reward.

A loving mother doesn't love her infant for any return, but simply because it is in her to love the child. A loving father doesn't love his son because he's a good basketball player or comes first in his schoolwork. Though this love seems most often expressed in family life, primarily in the love of parents for their children, it can and does commonly take other forms. It may be expressed in the love of children for their parents when the parents themselves become old and helpless. It may be expressed in the person who gives his or her life to some particular need of the human family, such as Mother Teresa choosing to live among the outcasts of Calcutta.

This love, I believe, is the highest expression of our humanity. No one level of love is wrong in itself, but the tragedy is that so many people never develop to mature love—they never grow beyond the self-centered concern of sexual or romantic desire. To grow in love from the most infantile level of sexual desire (*epithymia*), through the romantic desire of teen-age love (*eros*), to a responsible relationship in a mutual love (*philia*), and finally to the fullness of self-giving, sacrificial love (*agape*)— this is the way we develop to maturity, to the fullness of our humanity, and here find the deepest and most abiding happiness. Paradoxically, it is when we lose ourselves in the spirit of this love that we are most likely to find self-fulfillment.

The Love God Defines

The word *agape* was not commonly used in Greek custom. But when the writers of the New Testament looked for a word to describe the love of God in Jesus Christ, his living and dying, this is the one they chose as most suitable.

When the New Treatment says, "God is love," it means "God is *agape*" (1 John 4:8). God loves, not for gain or return, not because of anything admirable or loveable in us. God loves us, not because we are so loveable, but because God is love.

It is significant that Jesus spoke of God as *Abba*, a word we commonly translate as "father." Not that God is like us, but rather that, as a father, I am to love my children as God loves me. In Christ, we are called to love one another with the same love that we know in Christ. And this is that particular and peculiar quality that Christian faith has advocated as the highest of all human relationships, the love which God commands us to show one another, the love which is willing to turn the other cheek, to give without thought of return, to reach out to those who are helpless and in need, even those who are unloving and unlovable.

This quality of love is what the apostle Paul refers to in his famous "hymn to love":

> If I speak in the tongues of mortals and of angels, but do not have love, I am a noisy gong or a clanging cymbal. And if I have prophetic powers, and understand all mysteries and all knowledge, and if I have all faith, so as to remove mountains, but do not have love, I am nothing. If I give away all my possessions, and if I hand over my body so that I may boast, but do not have love, I gain nothing.
>
> Love is patient; love is kind; love is not envious or boastful or arrogant or rude. It does not insist on its own way; it is not irritable or resentful; it does not rejoice in wrongdoing, but rejoices in the truth. It bears all things, believes all things, hopes all things, endures all things. . . .
>
> And now faith, hope, and love abide, these three, and the greatest of these is love.

1 Corinthians 13:1–7, 13

When I was doing post-graduate study, I studied for a year with Paul Scherer, one of the great biblical preachers of the twentieth century. One spring Dr. Scherer was invited to preach at a "Flower Service" at an exclusive girl's school up the Hudson River from New York. He was asked to use as his text, "God is love."

Now Paul Scherer hated sentimentality, especially religious sentimentality. He was probably expected to preach about flowers and beauty and how nice it would be if everyone loved one another. Instead, he began his sermon by saying, "My text is 'God is love!'—not 'love is God!'" And he went on to preach on the cross.

> Let me read the text as it should be read, putting the emphasis where it belongs: not God is *love*, but *God* is love. When you say it that way, you are saying the costliest thing that could be said of God. You are not talking any longer simply of affection, of kindliness, of tender regard. . . . To say as the Bible says, "God so loved the world, that He gave His only begotten Son," is precisely in that measure, by all the width of the sky, different from saying that God is either fond of it or mildly amused by it. . . . Its symbol is the cross, where God has come to meet us under the very burden and weight of all our sin and suffering, in order that just there, by paying down on the counter of human life and human history the price of His own coming, He might give us the pledge of victory. . . . That's what genuine love is all about.[5]

"God is love" (1 John 4:8). I suppose many of us learned this short verse of Scripture at our mother's knee or in the very early years of Sunday school. What we have done, too often, is take these words and, assuming that we know what love is, say, "That's what God is like." But our understanding of love comes from the world around us. The result is not a definition of God, but a deification of love. "God is love" doesn't use our understanding of love to tell us what God is like, rather that God in Christ tells us what God's love is like. It tells us the love that God defines.

This passage goes on at once to say (v. 9): "God's love was revealed among us in this way: God sent his only Son into the world so that we might live through him. Immediately it then repeats it, as though to make sure we get it (v. 10): "In this is love, not that we loved God but that he loved us, and sent his Son to be the atoning sacrifice for our sins."

Agape is self-giving, unconditional, and unconcerned about whether it is rewarded. Here is a love, which is called out not because of the goodness or the beauty of the one who is loved, but because it is the very nature of the one who loves, even loves that which is unlovely and unlovable.

Think of how many ways in which the Bible keeps telling us this—the love that "does not insist on its own way" (1 Corinthians 13:5); that "makes his sun rise on the evil and on the good, and sends rain on the righteous and on the unrighteous" (Matthew 5:45); that "while we were still weak" suffered and died for us (Romans 5:6); and "God so loved that world that he gave . . ." (John 3:16). And in the Old Testament—"As a father has compassion for his children, so the Lord has compassion for those who fear him" (Psalm 103:13).

Swedish theologian Anders Nygren contrasts "human love" and "divine love":[6]

> Human love (*eros*) is—Acquisitive desire and longing; an upward movement, our effort to ascend to God; assumes that our salvation is our own work; egocentric love, a form of self-assertion of the highest kind; seeks to gain its own life, immortalized; wills to get and possess; is determined by and dependent upon the quality, beauty and worth of its object, is not spontaneous but is "evoked" by the *recognized value* in its object.
>
> Divine love (*agape*) is—sacrificial giving; God's way to us; unselfish love, which freely spends itself; dares to lose its life for the Gospel; freely gives and spends, dependent on God's love; is spontaneous, overflowing, unmotivated, and *creates value* in its object.

Yet, even as we use the word, as I try to define what it means, we must realize that to understand it we must look not at the word, what we may think it means, not what I say I think it means, but at Christ and at the cross! For it's not how we define love, but how God defines it. And it is at the cross of Christ that we see how God defines this love. It is my hope that you will turn to the Bible to know love, and that you will read it not for facts and figures but for the love of God.

We are well aware of the idolatry given by our culture to romantic love (*eros*), but we must also be aware of the possibility in

Christian faith that we make *agape* idolatrous by reducing it to a concept. It can be understood only in relationship to God in Christ, which is why we need to keep returning to "Square One," the Word.

God's grace is this love in action. "Knowing God" means entering into this love. Sin is the violation of this love. Righteousness is living in the spirit of this love in our relationship with God and with others.

The more we encounter the love of God through the Word of God, the more we will be transformed into the holiness of love. Holiness sends us out into the world to express that love in our living. As we return to the Word for our nourishment, respond in prayer, and seek God in worship, our faith is strengthened and the love of God becomes more real to us. Reading the Bible for the love of God will give us a bit of the shine of the radiance of God, the aroma of Christ, because we are looking for and responding to the Source of love. Reading the Bible for religious performance makes us legalistic like the Pharisees. Reading the Bible for love of God will bring us love, joy, and peace—the fruits of the Spirit (Galatians 5:22).

The holiness of love corrects our understanding of what it means to call Jesus "Lord"—not as one who holds power over us but the One who surrenders that power in humble service and sacrificial love. The glory and majesty of God come to focus not in power and might but in *agape,* love. "In the cross of Christ I glory!"

It is this same costly love to which we who are "created in God's image" are called—called to love without limit, even without thought or plan. "This is my commandment, that you love one another as I have loved you" (John 15:12). For "since God loved us so much, we also ought to love one another" (1 John 4:11). We love, not because we are going to get something out of it, not because it gets us into heaven, not because it's the right thing to do, but because God is love and by his Spirit we love one another. As the apostle Paul wrote, our model of love is Jesus Christ:

> Let Christ himself be your example as to what your attitude should be. For he, who had always been God by nature, did not cling to his prerogatives as God's equal, but stripped himself of all privilege by consenting to be a slave by nature and being born as mor-

tal man. And, having become man, he humbled himself by living a life of utter obedience, even to the extent of dying, *and the death he died was the death of a common criminal.*

Philippians 2:5–8 PHILLIPS (emphasis added)

That's the kind of love to which we are called—the kind of love that God defines. Don't assume that all that's expected of us is "little deeds of kindness, little words of love, that help to make life happy like the heaven above." A Christian lifestyle does not comprise a bit of charity here and there—spare cash for the poor or a few cans of beans for the soup kitchen. The love God defines demands all that we have—to love God with heart and soul and strength and mind, and our neighbors as ourselves.

We are still self-centered creatures. But insofar as we do live this *agape* in the Spirit of God, we begin to realize what it means to speak of love as the greatest thing in the world. It may seem strange to speak of something so demanding, so costly, and sometimes so painful as the greatest thing in the world. And yet those who have loved in this way, those who have loved their children beyond all limit and understanding, those who have loved others without return or reward, those who have given themselves to the service of human suffering for the love of God will understand and indeed will speak of it as "the greatest gift one can be given."

Frederick Buechner's novel *Brendan* is the story of Brendan the Navigator, an Irish monk who was born about 484 near Tralee, Ireland, and died some ninety years later. Brendan sailed the seas looking for souls to save. He built monasteries and nunneries and led a life of extreme asceticism and devotion in his endeavor to serve God.

Buechner's story is narrated by Finn, Brendan's fellow traveler and confidant. Late in the story, Brendan is still searching for "salvation." He has traveled to Wales to win souls for Christ and is staying with the monk Gildas, who "spent his days in his hut with a quill in his hand scratching out on his parchments the nastiness of his times."

Gildas and Brendan discuss their respective missions. Gildas believes his work is to record the sinners of his times and all their sins: "to set their names down here with all their sins written after them so the angels don't let a solitary one slip through their fingers." Brendan replies:

> "It was work for the poor Welsh folk I was thinking of rather."
>
> "We must pray for their souls surely," Gildas said, "My monks are at it day and night."
>
> "That's our monkish way, Father," Brendan said, "but the King of Heaven asks more of us than that, I think."
>
> "He asks from each of us what we have in us to give," Gildas said. "I've given so many years at these parchments my eyes have gone asquint. Doubtless you've done as much yourself from the looks of you."
>
> "Perhaps we've given all but what he truly wants," Brendan said.
>
> "And what is that, Father, if I may be so bold?" Gildas said. . . .
>
> "I only wish I knew for sure," Brendan said.
>
> Filling the walls of his cell with a mark for each soul he's won? Sailing the grim deserts of the sea? Starving himself into his grave nearly? Scattering monkeries and nun houses over the green earth like corn at spring planting? Was all that what Heaven wanted of him truly? Was any of that what Heaven wanted of him truly? The question he was asking himself was plain as the furrow between his brows.
>
> "He wants us each one to have a loving heart," Brendan said. The words come slowly. "When all's said and done, perhaps that's the length and the breadth of it."[7]

10

THE BIBLE FOR YOU
AND ME

A Prayer for Transformed Relationships

> For most of my life I have struggled to find God, to know God, to
> love God. . . . Now I wonder whether I have sufficiently realized
> that during all this time God has been trying to find me, to know
> me, to love me. . . . [The] question is not "How am I to love God?"
> but "How am I to let myself be loved by God?"
>
> Henri Nouwen[1]

It was more than fifty years ago that my search for God brought
me to the point of offering my life to God. Still unsure of any
sense of call, I decided that I would start studying theology and
see what happened from there.

I fought my whole family when I decided to leave the bank and
go into the ministry. My father had been a minister to rural
churches in the Maritime provinces of Canada through the 1930s
and my family all knew it was a hard life with not much in the
way of material rewards. My older brother wrote me a fifteen-
page letter trying to dissuade me from leaving "my financial
career" with its promise of success and security. My other brother
didn't speak to me for six months. Even my mother, devout Chris-

tian that she was, laid her hand on my arm and said, "Be sure it's what you want, son."

I left the bank because I wouldn't sell my soul to the Royal Bank of Canada. I found that the temptation to sell your soul to the United Church of Canada is just as strong and a lot more insidious. Back then, going to church was still the expected thing to do in the community. Churches were crowded Sunday mornings. If I put out an announcement for "Church Membership Classes," thirty or forty teenagers would show up. But it was a pretty shallow Christianity. In a congregation of a thousand families, there were only a very few people who would lead in public prayer. If I promoted a Bible study group, five or six would show up. In contrast, in my last congregation, a survey showed that about seventy-five percent of the congregation was involved in Bible study. We had an inspired and inspiring group of worship elders who would lead in prayer or conduct our worship service.

I am encouraged that there is a new sense in the churches of the centrality of the Bible. Many denominations are using lectionary readings and preaching is generally more biblical than the homilies of a few years ago on how to be successful or find peace of mind. Some were nothing more than lectures on social issues. Nominal Christianity is dead. If you don't mean it, you don't bother. Those people who choose to be "in" are more dedicated, more committed. They may not take the Bible literally, but they do take it seriously and struggle to relate it to their living. Others want in, but are put off by those whose understanding of the Bible is literalist or legalist. They want to read the Bible to experience and understand their relationship with God, not to get involved in disputes.

If we can become aware of this renewed hunger, perhaps we can avoid some of the disputes that have plagued the church for the last one hundred years. Living with the Bible in this way shapes us for relationships with others—with families, neighbors, even our enemies. To live in the love that Jesus revealed may not seem to be easy, but it is the way to a full, lasting, stable, and self-fulfilling life. And it seems to become ever more apparent that for our world today this is the only way to justice and peace.

It seems to me that among the truest words ever spoken or written were those of Augustine of Hippo when he wrote in his *Con-*

fessions, "Thou hast made us for Thyself, and our hearts are restless till they find their rest in Thee." Our hearts *are* restless. We want to know and experience God, to walk each day with a sense of God's presence and in the knowledge of God's love. We want to walk with God, not only "in the garden," but also in our family life, our work, our leisure. In the Bible as the Word of God, may we meet and hear the voice of the One who calls us into communion, in love.

It has been a wonderful thing to be a pastor, sharing the heights and depths of people's lives in birth, marriage, crisis, celebration, and death. But perhaps the most wonderful part is helping people to find faith. I pray that you have discovered in this book that the Bible truly is for *you*—for your encounter with God and your journey of living in love, that you may begin reading it for the love of God.

NOTES

Chapter 1

1. Walter Brueggemann, *The Bible Makes Sense* (Atlanta: John Knox, 1977), pp. 152–53.

2. Phyllis Trible, "Preaching luminaries tell pastors to oppose 'Bible-bashers, Bible-thumpers,'" http://www.wfn.org/2000/06/msg00051.html (2 June 2000).

3. See Fritjof Capra, *The Turning Point: Science, Society, and the Rising Culture* (New York: Bantam, 1988), p. 283–84.

4. Douglas Coupland, *Life After God* (New York: Simon and Schuster, 1994), p. 359.

5. Walter Wink, *The Bible in Human Transformation: Toward a New Paradigm for Bible Study* (Philadelphia: Fortress, 1973), p. 1.

6. Ibid., p. 1.

7. Karl Barth, "Strange New World within the Bible" in *The Word of God and the Word of Man*, trans. Douglas Horton (London: Hodder and Stoughton, 1928), pp. 28–50.

Chapter 2

1. Virginia Stem Owens, *And The Trees Clap Their Hands: Faith, Perception, and the New Physics* (Grand Rapids: Eerdmans, 1983), pp. 58–59. This book, which is now unfortunately out of print, is as poetic as it is scientific.

2. A remark by Monsignor Vincent Nichols, Archbishop of Birmingham, in a presentation at the National Consultation on "The Gospel and Contemporary Culture" at Swanwick in 1992. He was chairperson of the conference at that time.

3. Wolfgang Kohler, *The Place of Value in a World of Facts*, The William James Lectures on Philosophy and Psychology (New York: Liveright, 1938).

4. Lesslie Newbigin, *Foolishness to the Greeks: The Gospel and Modern Culture* (Grand Rapids: Eerdmans, 1986). Note also Lesslie Newbigin, *The Gospel in a Pluralist Society* (Grand Rapids: Eerdmans, 1989). These books are both well worth a good hard read.

5. Newbigin, *Foolishness to the Greeks*, p. 65.

6. Ibid., pp. 80–81. The quotation is Newbigin but the analysis is mine.

7. Matthew Arnold, "Stanzas from the Grande Chartreuse," lines 85–86.

8. Northrop Frye, *The Double Vision: Language and Meaning in Religion* (Toronto: United Church Publishing House, 1991), pp. 23–24. "There is a sense in which Blake was right. There is no God in the scientific vision as such."

9. Quoted in David Suzuki and Holly Dressel, *From Naked Ape to Superspecies* (Toronto and New York: Stoddart, 1999), p. 15.

10. Note Jacob Bronowski, *The Common Sense of Science* (Cambridge, Mass.: Harvard University Press, 1978), p. 78.

11. Michael Polanyi, *Personal Knowledge: Towards a Post-Critical Philosophy* (Chicago: University of Chicago Press, 1962), p. vii.

12. Einstein himself, with his great awe of the order of the universe, had a firm belief in God—a God responsible for the order of it all. He found great difficulty in accepting Heisenberg's "Principle of Uncertainty." "God does not play dice," he remarked. But Einstein could find no place for a personal God. The law of the universe left no place for an arbitrary "Providence." But to say that God is a person does not necessarily deny the faithfulness of God. See Albert Einstein, *Ideas and Opinions,* Laurel Edition (New York: Dell, 1981), pp. 56–57.

Chapter 3

1. Karl Barth, *The Word of God and the Word of Man* (Gloucester, Mass.: Peter Smith, 1978), p. 42. Emphasis in the original.

2. Until the twentieth century, the terms Protestant and evangelical had very much the same meaning.

3. Note Karen Armstrong's book *The Battle for God* (New York: Knopf, 2000), pp. 135ff., for an accurate history and sympathetic evaluation.

4. Robert M. Grant with David Tracy, *A Short History of the Interpretation of the Bible,* 2d ed. (Philadelphia: Fortress, 1984), p. 129.

5. Harry Emerson Fosdick, *The Living of these Days: An Autobiography* (New York: Harper and Brothers, 1956), p. 145.

6. Ibid.

7. The historical inaccuracies of both the play and the movie are noted in Edward Larson, *Summer for the Gods* (Cambridge, Mass.: Harvard University Press, 1998).

8. Peterson has now translated the whole of the Bible. He says, in his introduction to the New Testament, that he seeks to present the Bible "in a contemporary idiom [that] keeps the language of the Message current and fresh and understandable in the same language in which we do our shopping, talk with our friends, worry about world affairs, and teach our children their table manners." Eugene H. Peterson, *The Message: The Bible in Contemporary Language* (Colorado Springs: NavPress, 2002), p. 1742.

9. Eugene H. Peterson, "Back to Square One: God Said!" in *Subversive Spirituality*, Jim Lyster, John Sharon, Peter Santucci, eds. (Grand Rapids/Vancouver: Eerdmans/Regent College, 1994, 1997), pp. 30–31.

10. Martin Buber, *I and Thou* (New York: Scribner's, 1970), p. 156.

Chapter 4

1. For a brief background, see Thomas Edward Frank, *Polity, Practice and the Mission of the United Methodist Church* (Nashville: Abingdon, 1997), p. 134.

2. Edward George Bulwer-Lytton, *Richelieu* (1839), II.ii.

3. Northrup Frye, *The Great Code: The Bible and Literature* (New York: Harcourt Brace Jovanovich, 1982), p. 200.

Chapter 5

1. Donald Bloesch, *Essentials of Evangelical Theology: God, Authority, and Salvation* (New York: Harper and Row, 1978), vol. 1, pp. 62–63.

2. "In this period, there is relatively little emphasis on a clear separation of subject and object: the emphasis falls rather on the feeling that subject and object are linked by a common power or energy. Many 'primitive' societies have words expressing this common energy of human personality and natural environment, which are untranslatable into our normal categories of thought but are very pervasive in theirs." Frye, *The Great Code*, p. 6.

3. "The criterion of truth is related to the external source of the description rather than to the inner consistency of the argument," Frye, *The Great Code*, p. 13.

4. Note Frye, *The Great Code*, chapter I, "Language I," pp. 3–30.

5. Luci Shaw, "How to Enter a Poem," in *The Angels Of Light: New and Selected Poems* (Wheaton, Ill.: Shaw, 2000), p. 11.

6. "History and Myth in the Bible," a talk originally given to the English Institute in New York. See Alvin A. Lee and Jean O'Grady, eds., *Northrop Frye on Religion*, vol. 4 (Toronto: University of Toronto Press, 2000), pp. 10–22.

7. Ibid., pp. 17 and 19.

8. Ibid., pp. 20–21

9. Karen Armstrong, in *The Battle for God,* has a similar distinction between *mythos* and *logos* that is also helpful. See p. xiii, etc.

10. "Which beginning of time according to our Chronologie, fell upon the entrance of the night preceding the twenty third day of Octob. In the year of the Julian Calendar, 710 (i.e., 4004 BC)." Archbishop James Ussher, *The Annals of the World* (1658), p. 1.

11. Robert McAfee Brown, *The Bible Speaks to You* (Philadelphia: Westminster, 1955), pp. 60–61. Note especially the first four chapters.

12. If the above division of truth seems to you to smack of schizophrenia, I agree. Surely truth is finally one. But it is a common and seemingly reputable distinction we have made. Aristotle made it for one, and Leibnitz also distinguished between "rational (necessary) truth" and "empirical (contingent) truth."

13. George Adam Smith's commentary on Jonah in *The Expositor's Bible,* F. W. Robertson Nicoll, ed. (New York: A. C. Armstrong & Sons, 1908).

14. Eugene H. Peterson, *Leap Over A Wall: Earthy Spirituality for Everyday Christians* (San Francisco: HarperCollins, 1997), p 5.

15. Ibid., p. 5.

16. William Barclay, The Gospel of John in *The Daily Study Bible* (Edinburgh: St. Andrew's Press, 1955), I:80

Chapter 6

1. Charlotte Elliott, "Just as I Am" in *The United Methodist Hymnal: Book of United Methodist Worship* (Nashville: United Methodist Publishing House, 1989), no. 357.

2. John Greenleaf Whittier, "The Eternal Goodness" in *The Poetical Works of John Greenleaf Whittier with Notes, Biographical, Critical, and Explanatory,* William Michael Rossetti, ed. (London: Ward, Lockard, n.d.), pp. 397–98.

3. W. H. Auden, "For the Time Being: A Christmas Oratorio" in *The Collected Poetry of W. H. Auden* (New York: Random House, 1945), p. 457.

4. A. E. Bailey, *The Gospel in Hymns* (New York: Charles Scribner's Sons, 1950), p. 183.

5. In *Under the Unpredictable Plant* (Grand Rapids: Eerdmans, 1992), Peterson writes, "I would prefer not to use the term 'spiritual director'" (p. 177). Note pp. 187–88, which explains his use of the term and his hesitation.

6. Ibid., p. 90.

7. From John Ayto, *Dictionary of Word Origins* (New York: Arcade/Little, Brown, 1990), p. 107.

Chapter 7

1. Frye, *The Great Code*, p. xii.
2. Choruses from "The Rock," VI, T. S. Eliot, *The Complete Poems and Plays, 1909-1950* (New York: Harcourt, Brace and World, 1952), p. 106.
3. The Church of England, 1662, the collect for the second Sunday of Advent.
4. Eugene H. Peterson, *Eat This Book* (Vancouver: Regent College Publishing, 2000), p. 12.
5. "You must strive hard and struggle—you must groan, you must agonize, why you must pray till your nose bleeds, or it will not avail." Quoted by William G. McLoughlin Jr. in *Modern Revivalism: Charles Grandison Finney to Billy Graham* (New York: Ronald Press, 1959), p. 27.
6. Walter Rauschenbusch, "The Little Gate to God," in *Masterpieces of Religious Verse*, ed. James Dalton Morrison (New York: Harper and Brothers, 1948), pp. 72–73.
7. William Barclay, *A New Testament Wordbook* (London: SCM, 1955), p. 35.
8. Paul Scherer, "Now About the Church," in *Facts that Undergird Life* (New York: Harper, 1938), pp. 178–80—language changed slightly!
9. Note John Calvin, *Institutes of the Christian Religion*, IV, xiv, 1, 3, and 17.
10. Luci Shaw, *God in the Dark: Through Grief and Beyond* (Grand Rapids: Zondervan, 1989), p. 73.
11. Peter Shaffer, *Equus* (Markham, Ontario: Penguin, 1981), Act II, 25, p. 82.
12. Ibid., Act I, 1, p. 17.
13. Michael Polanyi, *Personal Knowledge*, p. 405.
14. Ibid., p. 198.

Chapter 8

1. Quoted by William G. McLoughlin Jr., *Modern Revivalism: Charles Grandison Finney to Billy Graham*. Note pp. 84–100.
2. Meanipulation is a harsh word, but revivalism is open to this charge. Note William McLoughlin, "Specialists in the Engineering of Mass Consent" in *Modern Revivalism*.
3. Note Timothy Smith, *Revivalism and Social Reform in Mid-Nineteenth Century America* (New York: Abingdon, 1957). Note David O. Moberg, *The Great Reversal: Evangelism versus Social Concern* (Philadelphia: J. B. Lippincott, 1972). Moberg notes that Timothy Smith was the one who originated the term "the Great Reversal."
4. "The Church and Evangelism in a Day of Revolution," *Christianity Today* 14 (24 October 1969), pp. 6–12.

5. Note Leighton Ford, *One Way to Change the World* (New York: Harper and Row, 1970).

6. Karl Barth, *The Faith Of The Church: A Commentary on the Apostles' Creed according to Calvin's Catechism*, ed. Jean-Louis Leuba, trans. Gabriel Vahanian (London and Glasgow: Fontana Books/Meridian Books, 1958), p. 122. Note this section on "The Task of the Church."

7. Dietrich Bonhoeffer, *The Cost of Discipleship* (London: SCM, 1959), from the opening paragraphs of Article I, pp. 35f.

8. T. S. Eliot, *Complete Poems and Plays*, choruses from "The Rock," p. 106.

9. Rudolf Otto, *The Idea of the Holy* (Oxford: Oxford University Press, 1931).

10. "There is an imperative, which, irrespective of every ulterior end or aim, command categorically." Immanuel Kant, *The Metaphisic of Ethics*, trans. J. W. Semple, 3d ed. (Edinburgh: T & T Clark, 1871), p. 29.

11. "Two things fill the mind with ever new and increasing admiration and awe, the oftener and the more steady we reflect upon them: *the starry heavens above and the moral law within.*" (Immanuel Kant, *The Critique of Practical Reason* in *Great Books of the Western World,* ed. Robert Maynard Hutchins (Chicago, London, Toronto, Geneva, Sydney, Tokyo: Encyclopaedia Britannica), p. 360.

12. Quoted by Reinhold Niebuhr in a sermon, "The Providence of God," *Justice and Mercy,"* ed. Ursula M. Niebuhr (New York: Harper and Row, 1976), p. 15.

13. Dag Hammerskjold, *Markings* (London: Faber and Faber, 1964). He once said, "I inherited a belief that no life is more satisfactory than one of self-less service."

14. George Macleod, *Only One Way Left* (Glasgow, Iona, Edinburgh: The Iona Community, 1956), p. 38.

Chapter 9

1. Eugene H. Peterson, "Introduction to 1, 2, & 3 John," *The Message: New Testament, Psalms, and Proverbs in Contemporary Language* (Colorado Springs: NavPress, 1995), p. 503.

2. Note Erich Fromm, *The Art of Loving* (New York: Harper and Brothers, 1956), pp. 1–6—an old but still a good book and worth reading.

3. Note Denys de Rougement, *Love in the Western World* (New York: Pantheon Books, 1956), a fascinating thesis that romantic love is essentially self-love and ultimately leads to self-destruction.

4. Fromm, *The Art of Loving*, p. 22.

5. Paul Scherer, "The Love That God Defines!" in *The Word God Sent* (New York: Harper and Row, 1965), pp. 225–33.

6. Anders Nygren, *Agape and Eros* (London: SPCK, 1953), p. 210.

7. Frederick Buechner, *Brendan* (New York: Atheneum, 1987), pp. 209ff.

Chapter 10

1. Henri Nouwen, *The Return of the Prodigal Son* (New York: Double-day/Image, 1992), p. 106.